WIDE BOY

WIDE BOY

Montague Bentley

Published in 2005 by 30° South Publishers (Pty) Ltd.
28, 9th Street, Newlands, 2092
Johannesburg, South Africa
www.30degreessouth.co.za
info@30degreessouth.co.za

Dictionary definitions courtesy *Oxford Advanced Learner's Dictionary*, 4th Edition, 1989
Design and origination by Kerrin Cocks
Printed and bound by Pinetown Printers (Pty) Ltd.

ISBN 0-9584890-7-6

I am an opportunist. I take advantage of any opportunity to achieve an end, often with no regard for principles or consequences. In a world where money and fame are held above all, success is gauged by your cars, your home, your clothes … and your women. This is the world of the opportunist—ripe with chance, rich with possibility—and, above all, amoral.

My name is Tony Meyer, but Montague Bentley has more of a ring to it—more in keeping with my status.

Montague Bentley
Johannesburg, 2005

Chapter
One

The African sun shone hard and bright, searing the tar beneath his feet. Tony sighed, the day was far too hot for his liking and all he wanted to do was bury himself in the cool waters of the local pool. He was average height for a kid his age, ten years old, with a mop of curly brown hair that fell in his eyes on a regular basis. Long skinny legs shot out from beneath his khaki pants and ended in white socks and khaki veldskoene. He was on his way to the local Greek café to buy some groceries for his Ma with a crisp curl of pound notes in his pocket. As he turned the comer onto Main Street a group of tough Afrikaners got up from the low wall beside the road.

"Hey! You!" yelled one, a strapping lad with thick beefy arms and a puffed-out chest. He was the leader of the group, they called him *'Ag nee'* (oh no), and the name was well deserved. This was the local Bez Valley gang of boys who took great pleasure in beating up anyone or anything smaller than them, unfortunate enough to wander across their path. Sadly, today it was Tony's turn to get a black nose or a blue eye and he was definitely not in the mood. Last week he'd managed to outrun them—it hadn't been that hard, after all, they were big and ungainly while he was fast and built like a whippet.

Tony stopped dead in the centre of the pavement, his arms hanging loosely by his side, as the five of them sauntered over.

"Where ya off to, midget?" sneered Agnee. "Off to buy a dress?"

Tony didn't answer but he started to loosen his muscles slowly, one by one, preparing them for the sprint ahead. But this time they had planned for his usual form of escape as three of the lugs circled behind him, closing off all his escape routes.

"Well?" Agnee shoved Tony hard in the chest, forcing him to totter backwards into the arms of Theo and Tobie behind him. They grabbed hold of his skinny appendages and pulled him apart.

"Not so fast and furious now, are we?" Agnee smirked at the terror on Tony's face. "Think you can get away from this, huh?"

Tony felt as if his stomach was about to hit the floor; there was no way he was going to escape from this situation without a severe bruising and he'd probably end up losing his mother's shopping money as well. Nor could they could afford to lose the precious pounds in his pocket. His father's store had burnt down in a fire and he'd lost everything. Now, while he was looking for another job, things were very tight in the Meyer household.

"Oi!" a strident voice cried out from somewhere behind the group. "Oi! What are you boys doing, eh?"

It was Mr Stanopolous, the owner of the Greek store, standing behind them with his hands on his hips. Agnee turned and his face underwent a remarkable change. From the sneering, ugly growl that had been etched into his bullying face there was now a look of horror. Agnee snapped his fingers and Tony found himself falling to the ground as the two thugs let him go and the entire band raced off into the distance.

"You alright there, lad?" asked Mr Stanoplous kindly; he'd seen the trapped look on Tony's face and knew that no kid would have enjoyed whatever grief Agnee and his gang had planned for him.

Tony shook his head briefly to clear it before standing up.

"Actually I'm fine. Thanks, Mr Stanopolous. You sure came along at a good time there."

"Those boys ..." Mr Stanopolous shook his head slowly. "They'll get themselves into some real trouble soon. I just hope it's not too late. Personally I blame the parents. Not a one of them cares a damn for these boys. Leaving them all alone to find their own way." He turned his massive bulk and trod heavily back towards the cool interior of his shop. Tony watched him walk. He was a short man with straight black hair oiled down over his pate and the most impressive thing about him was his size. Stan Stanopolous was about as wide as he was tall and something of a local celebrity because of this. Tony found it amazing that he could walk at all.

After a moment his body shook off the vague effects of the shock that the Agnee gang had inflicted and the relentless heat of the African sun drew him towards the air-conditioned shop.

A bright red sign proclaimed in white print 'Stan's Tea Room' as it hung above the door. An ice-cream machine sat and coughed outside. Beneath the awning was pinned a fluttering paper, asking all those who took an ice-cream to pay on their honour. Stan believed that all people were basically good and so he placed a great deal of trust in them. He also kept a beady eye on it whenever the school kids were about because he knew that they hadn't quite developed a conscience just yet.

Tony bent over the machine with a glint in his eye. Chocolate ices—the perfect way to drop the internal thermostat to bearable levels in the summer heat but first, shopping.

It didn't take him long to collect the eggs, milk and sugar that were on his Ma's list. Nor did it take him long to steal at least three chocolates, a handful of cherry pops and a Coca-Cola. Tony felt that he was probably one of the best shoplifters in Bez Valley, if not Johannesburg itself. Carefully and cleverly he hid the various items all over his body so that neither a lump nor a bump showed itself to the casual observer. The first three times he'd slipped something small into his pocket or knapsack he'd gone to the counter sweating with fear of getting caught. He'd flinched every time Mr Stanopolous had asked him a question or handed him his change. After that it had been a matter of the greatest of ease. The morality issue didn't concern him in the slightest. It never had. It was about wanting something and taking it—that was what life was all about and he was simply starting with some little things to see him by. After all, Mr Stanopolous wouldn't even notice the loss, and if he did, that was his problem after all. It was his decision to run a business, wasn't it?

"Here you go, Mr Stanopolous," said Tony as he offloaded the contents of the shopping list onto the counter. "I hope there's enough change for a chocolate ice. It's really hot out there."

Stan stared piercingly at Tony. He wasn't entirely sure about this kid. Seemed nice enough on the outside—always polite and cheerful, never hanging with a bad crowd, but there was something about him that seemed a little, well, off.

Still, you couldn't run about glaring at people on the basis of a hunch, so Stan shrugged his shoulders and started to ring up the various items.

Ten minutes later Tony was happily ensconced on a wall, overlooking the river, sucking on his chocolate ice and sipping on his purloined Coke. Both tasted great because he hadn't had to pay a cent and neither was going to get him into trouble, as he'd got away with it, again.

On the other hand he really needed to figure out a way to handle the Agnee gang. They were starting to become a major pain and he had no idea what to do. He sat pondering. After a while an idea came to him. He'd go and visit Mad Uncle Mick—his seven-foot, muscle-bound wrestler of an uncle who lived in the same neighbourhood. Maybe he could persuade his burly uncle to come with him to school one day and frighten the daylights out of those stupid boys.

It was a perfect plan.

A low whistle startled Tony from his delighted reverie.

"Hey, Tony!" a soft voice whispered in his ear. "How about sharing some of that chocolate ice? It looks super cold and I'm really dying of heat here."

Tony grinned as he turned to look into the bright blue eyes of Janna Maitland. She was one of the two girls in their little group at school and definitely the prettiest. Her shortish brown hair was swept up into two tiny little pigtails from which most had already escaped and was now hanging into her face and brushing the sides of her pert little nose.

"First a kiss," he winked and pushed out his lips.

"Sis! You look like a duck's bottom when you do that!" she shrieked, half scandalized and half pleased. She also thought that Tony was terribly cute and rather liked his insistence on kissing her at every opportunity. She couldn't let him know that though.

"Aw, come on Jan, just a little one. Here! On my cheek?"

"Hmm," she said, pretending to ponder the issue; swinging back and forth on one heel. "Alright. But I get at least three licks of the ice!"

"Deal!"

Tony grabbed her by both arms. Not a very romantic gesture, but he was young yet, and kissed her soundly on the mouth.

"TONY!" she gasped, jumping back a few steps. You said on the cheek!"

"Ah Janna, Janna ... you know I could never keep a promise like that."

"Give me the ice." She sounded petulant and she felt it. Sometimes Tony pushed just a little too hard and she didn't want him to think he could get away with it when it came to her. In her ten-year-old mind she had big plans for him and it was best she trained him early on.

Tony cheekily slipped the stick into her hand as he pulled two of the cherry pops from his bag.

"Tony! Where did you get those from? Surely you couldn't have bought them all out of your pocket money? You don't get that much."

"Why, Mr Stanopolous gave them to me, of course."

"GAVE them to you?" she said with disbelief.

"Well, yes," Tony feigned hurt. "Stan saved me from the Agnee gang and gave me a couple of cherry pops. Said it would take away the shock."

The news of the Agnee gang had the effect he'd anticipated. Janna completely forgot about the stolen sweets and dived straight into the subject of the neighbourhood gang. "They are the most disgusting idiots!" she exclaimed. "And they really have their eye on you. Why do they always pick on you?"

"They pick on everyone."

"Yes they do." Janna chewed her lip thoughtfully. "But they seem to look out for you. If you know what I mean."

Tony shrugged. "Dunno. I'm not bothered about it."

"Oh puhlease! I saw you running for your life last week."

"Kak man!"

"Oh. So it wasn't you sprinting across Ma Engelbrecht's lawn and flattening her hydrangeas?"

"Umm ... well ..."

Tony remembered the trouble he'd landed in and the fact that he now had to mow her lawn, every Saturday, for a month as punishment.

"Yeah, exactly!" crowed Janna triumphantly. Then she really studied his expression and her elation slipped away. "It's bad isn't it?"

"Yeah. Today they managed to block me off so I couldn't escape. The double-Ts, Theo and Tobie, they grabbed my arms. I don't know how bad it would've been if Stan hadn't arrived."

"Whew!" whistled Janna through her teeth. "That's very bad. What are you going to do?"

"I was thinking of asking Uncle Mick."

"Mad Uncle Mick?"

"The very one. If nothing else, maybe he'll come to school with me and give them a bit of a fright. That should do the trick."

Janna tilted her head to one side as she considered this. "It may work but you may find that it'll only make it worse."

Tony shrugged, "Oh well, it couldn't hurt to try. Anyway, I better get this stuff back to Ma. I'll see you later at Ian's place."

Tony jumped off the wall and headed off towards home. Carefully avoiding all the Agnee gang's usual hangout spots.

Bez Valley in 1943 was a beautiful place. The cars gleamed in the sun and the world was green with beautiful, big trees lining the streets. The walk home took him over a little river that ran along the main street and past some lovely old houses.

"Hey Ma!" he yelled as he came through the door of their neatly kept semi. Flowerboxes lined the front windows, filled with pansies, violets and others that Tony didn't know. A little cobblestone path, one that his Ma had browbeaten his father into finishing up last winter, led to the pale-yellow front door set into red face-brick.

"In here, Tony," his mother shouted from the kitchen. Tony carried the paper bag into the white linoleum kitchen where his mother was busy preparing dinner.

"Just put the bag on the table, dear," she smiled at him as she smoothly diced a carrot for the stew. "Everything go okay?"

"Yeah, fine Ma," he replied as he edged towards the door. He wasn't really in the mood for one of her bonding chats this afternoon. He still wanted to go and see his uncle before it got dark and his uncle had had too many gin and sodas.

"I'm going to visit Uncle Mick now, Ma. If that's okay," he added as an afterthought.

"Sure. But please take Aunt May some of the grapes that your father bought last week. They're not going to last much longer and I'm sure she'll appreciate them."

"Aw Ma," he moaned, knowing that he was making things worse for himself by whining.

Chapter
Two

Twenty minutes later Tony arrived at his uncle's house, laden down with fruit, flowers and even some clean laundry that his mother had done for her sister. His face was a picture of grumpiness. Next time, he vowed to himself, I will keep my big mouth shut!

"Tony! How nice to see you!" Aunt May opened the door as he clumped up the pathway.

"Your mother phoned and told me you were on your way. Can I offer you some lemonade? It's icy cool."

"Yes please," gasped Tony. Even at four in the afternoon, the African summer heat was stifling.

"Come on in," she held the door for him as he tottered in with his load.

"Thanks," he managed.

"Here. Put all those things on the table over there," Aunt May gestured towards the pine kitchen table. A shrine to all things clean and sparse. It always struck Tony as odd that his almost insane uncle lived with such a neat and, well, good woman. His aunt was the complete opposite to her husband. She was a tiny, thin woman with slender hands and long wavy brown hair that was always swept up into a style both complicated and efficient. While not ravishingly beautiful, she had the kind of face that seemed to glow when she smiled. Her dark brown eyes glinted at him now.

"Here's your drink, dear." She smiled, "Now go and find your uncle. He's outside on the verandah. Oh, and take him a refill won't you?"

Tony quickly whipped up a very weak gin and soda for his uncle, just in case, and wandered through to the garden.

"Hey, Uncle Mick, how're you doing?"

"Heeey! Tony! This is a nice surprise, and a drink to go with it. Excellent!"

His uncle had cushioned his huge bulk on a wrought-iron garden chair overlooking a well-tended garden. Bougainvillea crept along the walls beside flowering rose bushes and green, green grass. The hiss and spit of sprinklers, working from garden to garden, was a constant background noise.

"So, sonny, how's life treating you?"

"Fair to middling, Uncle Mick." There was a momentary pause. Suddenly Tony was unsure how to raise the subject of bullying with his uncle. After all, the man stood over six feet tall, was loaded with muscle and brooked no argument. Tony felt vaguely embarrassed. Fortunately he was saved the trouble as Mick launched into the story of what happened to him the previous day.

"I've been dying to tell you this, Tone. Yesterday I had one helluva hullabaloo."

"Really?" Tony's eyes widened. His uncle was renowned in the family for doing all sorts of insane things outside of the wrestling arena. Tony personally believed that all the aggression and machismo of the ring was difficult to control when faced with the normality of the outside world. He was known as 'Mick the Monster' and wore a bright purple and red outfit on stage. He had a big Star of David sewn onto the back of his cape, which he flaunted at the Afrikaner men who attended the wrestling matches. It was an act designed to provoke his opponents into a mad rage that would stop them from thinking clearly. And it worked. There was a lot of prejudice in the 1940s' South Africa and it wasn't only focused on the black population either. The Afrikaners who ran the country didn't like anyone or anything that contradicted their fundamental beliefs. Tony idolized his uncle for his open belief in the Jewish culture and his determination to stand up for who he was, no matter what.

"... there were at least three ways to do it."

Tony realized that he'd drifted off and had missed half of Mick's story.

"Sorry, uncle, I didn't catch the first part."

"Mind wandering, eh? Well that's fine. Where was I? Oh yes, I was driving back from training yesterday taking the usual route. You know? The one through Main Street?"

Tony nodded.

"Well, as I was heading up the hill this idiot comes driving up the other way in his brand-new Pontiac. The bastard took up near the entire road! So I moved over to the left a bit, to give him a bit of space to move. I mean, there were at least three ways he could get around me! If he knew how to drive that is." Mick took a deep swig from his nearly empty glass and looked vaguely mystified that his drink had finished so quickly. "He has the nerve to honk at me! Honk! At me! Well that was it. So I pulled back over to the right so he had nowhere to go and stopped. Right there in the middle of the road."

Tony nodded encouragingly. This was definitely looking up to be one of his uncle's better stories.

"Well, this chappie just sat in his car waving his arms at me and hitting that horn while I simply sat and stared at him over the wheel of my truck. Next thing I just got mad. There's this skinny little nobody yelling at me. ME! In the middle of Main Street and expecting me to get out of his way. So I slammed the truck into reverse. To give me a little running room you see," Mick winked at his nephew who sat staring at him with wide eyes, "and then I revved that truck in first gear harder than it's ever been pushed before and I drove straight into that bastard as fast as I could go."

Mick started laughing, "Man, he just sat there as he watched me come at him with these big eyes full of disbelief. I don't believe for one minute that he thought I would actually hit his shiny little car. Then I slammed the truck into reverse and did it again and again. Oh, son," Mick wiped the tears of laughter from his eyes, "You should have seen what was left of his car by the time I was done. The fender hanging off on one side, glass all over the road and his pretty little bonnet all crumpled up. Ha ha ha, you should have seen it. It was only after the third or fourth time that I rammed his car that he realized what was going on and tried to get his car off the road but, by that time, it was too late. That engine wasn't going anywhere."

"What did he do?" asked Tony breathlessly. This was even better than the last story.

"He got out that wrecked piece of crap, white as a sheet he was, waving his skinny arms and shouting who knows what. I decided to take pity on him, so I stopped and got out the truck, which, by the way, had hardly any damage. Your aunt isn't too impressed with me but it won't cost more than a couple of pounds to fix. You should have seen this little man's face when I got out. He turned tail and ran. I bet you can still see glass on that part of the road if you're of the mind."

Tony immediately made a mental note to take the gang up to Main Street to check for broken glass. It would be so cool to keep some in memory of this momentous event.

"That's amazing, Uncle Mick. So he didn't even try and talk to you?"

"Not a chance. I reckon the guy figured I'd do the same damage to him as I did to his car. But you didn't come down here to hear a story, now did you?

"Well," Tony hedged.

"Come on now, you came down here on a mission. Let's hear it."

Tony looked down at his feet. He wasn't sure how he should describe the situation. If he was honest, he was sure he'd look as foolish as the man whose car his uncle had destroyed the previous day but if he weren't then he wouldn't get a real solution to his problem. He sighed and made his decision. He really needed his uncle's help.

"Okay, well, I kinda need your help with something."

"Tell it to me straight, sonny."

So Tony told him everything, from the regular beatings to the more recent events, while his uncle sat and listened carefully to every word. They were interrupted only briefly by Aunt May bringing out more drinks and some snacks, which they both tucked into with pleasure.

When Tony was done Mick leant back in his chair and stared up at the darkening sky. The silence drew on and, for a moment, Tony thought his uncle had lost all respect for him. As if a nephew of his should never experience a problem like this.

"Right. Now, listen carefully Tony. My father told me this once, many years back, when I was in the same situation as you."

Tony stared at Mick in disbelief.

His uncle noted his expression and laughed, "Oh yes, I was also bullied at school. In fact most people are."

"I just find it hard to believe."

"Well, we all have our secrets. Let's just keep this one between us shall we?" Mick tapped the side of his nose conspiratorially.

"This is what you need to do. Whenever these boys come to you next, you need to walk right up to the head chap. The one that gives the orders, see?"

Tony nodded.

"Then you ask him, 'Do you want to hit me?' and you stare at him, right between the eyes. You stare at him with no fear and you ask him this question. The moment he moves, tries to hit you, or anything like it, you kick him hard in the balls." Uncle Mick leant close to Tony, his gin-scented breath brushing his cheek, "Now mark this well. Tony, you kick this boy as hard as you can. Don't run, don't say anything, just kick."

"But …"

"No buts. Just do it. It'll work, don't you worry about it."

"How … ?"

"Do you trust me, Tony?"

"Yes of course!"

"Then you go right ahead and do this tomorrow, the day after, or whenever. You do this. Then you come back to me and tell me if you still have a problem with these boys."

"Are you sure you can't just come with me to school, you know, scare them off a little?"

"I won't do your dirty work for you, Tony. This here's a moment when you make the decision as to what kind of man you want to be. Do you want to be a nancy who expects everyone to handle difficult situations for him or do you want to be an opportunist? A man who takes the moment with both hands and takes advantage of it to the best of his ability?"

Tony stared hard at his uncle.

"Now, it's getting late and my supper is ready as will be yours. Time for you to be off and back to your mam."

Tony realized that he wasn't going to get anything more from his uncle that day and despondently said his goodbyes and started the half-mile walk back home. As he walked he kicked a recalcitrant stone ahead of him, taking all his frustrations out on the dead rock. He couldn't believe that his uncle had given him such pointless advice. If he was big enough to take Agnee and his gang on by fist, then he would've done it ages ago. Now his last hope of finding relief had told him to go ahead and get himself killed. Tony was positive that the moment the words were out of his mouth Agnee would order his goons to crunch him into pulp. He also realized that he had no choice but to take his uncle's advice. There was no way he'd be able to look his uncle in the eye and lie to him. I'm in more trouble than I was before, he thought wryly.

By the time he got home, twilight was settling into night and the smell of his mother's stew filled the house. A hat and a suitcase beside the door testified to his father being home, so Tony went through to the kitchen to say hello.

"Hey Dad."

"Hey, son. How was school?"

"Oh, the usual. Boring."

"You need to pay more attention to your classes, Tony," his father lectured. It was an old discussion, done to death by daily repetition. Tony wasn't interested or good at school. In fact, the only reason he ever passed anything was because he copied every last word from his friend who sat beside him. He hated reading; writing was even worse and he honestly believed that everything he had learned was about as useful as learning how to knit. Tony believed, with his heart and soul, that he was destined for something more. That he could create great things outside of the system that ruled the world. "Yes, Dad," he replied in a monotone, anything to break the cycle. "How was your day?"

"It went really well."

"Yes, your father got a great job today," said his mother brightly. Only his father didn't look as excited.

"That's great. When do you start?"

"Started already today. Selling carpets. It's a wonderful opportunity."

Even Tony could pick up on the hollowness of his father's cheerfulness. It hadn't been like this in the past, before the store burnt down. Now they were scraping the bottom of the barrel and he could hear the defeat in his voice. His father was too old to start afresh at the foot of the ladder and was forced to take anything he could get to keep his family together.

"Carpets? That sounds interesting."

"It is, they're definitely very good quality. I have to drive around all day. Guess this'll give me a good chance to see the whole of Johannesburg."

"But, honey!" exclaimed his wife, "You can't ..."

"I know that, Laura. They've arranged a driver for me, a man called Windsor. They'll dock a portion of my salary for him, for sure, but they really made a plan."

His father couldn't drive and would never try to either. He ended up giving a portion of his salary every month to the black man, Windsor, who would take him wherever he needed to go. Another nail in his working coffin.

Tony sighed inwardly; he hated the fact that his father worked long and hard only to keep them at the basic level of survival. It was starting to form a burr in his chest. A burr that would never go away.

Chapter
Three

The following morning rose bright and cheerful. The sun shone through a gap in his brown curtains forcing Tony to wake up. His first thoughts were of the Agnee gang and what he had to do that day. He wondered if he could pretend to be sick. His mother would certainly let him stay home; he was hardly ever ill. No, he thought, I have to do this—if not today, then tomorrow and there is nothing I can do to make this go away except to face it head on.

He jumped out of bed and did his usual morning wake-up routine; brushing teeth, bathing, polishing his shoes. He then threw his school uniform on and wandered downstairs to breakfast.

"Hi Mom," he said, fairly subdued.

"What's wrong, honey? You okay?" His mother pressed the back of her hand against his forehead to see if he had a temperature. "You don't seem to be hot."

"Nah, I'm fine. Just tired, that's all."

"Well, don't stay too late after school with those friends of yours, then. I think a nice early night will do it for you."

Tony cursed inwardly. His mother was a typical Jewish mom who constantly worried about her son's health and happiness and now he'd have to come home earlier than he'd planned. He wanted to take his friends to look for glass where his uncle had rammed the unfortunate businessman, if the Agnee gang didn't destroy him first, that is.

"David will be home tomorrow, isn't that great?"

David was Tony's elder brother and a complete waste of time in his books. Quiet, shy and a loner, David was the antithesis of his brother. In fact, even Tony's friends didn't really know what to make of him, either. David would study hard and his only cool factor seemed to be that he liked sports, which was where he was at the moment. David had been chosen, along with five others, to represent their school at a sports festival. He'd been gone for five blissful days. Tony was dreading the usual rituals of 'Take care of your brother' and 'Why don't you take David with you?' He often had to take him with when he went out with his friends but that usually meant that he'd dump his bother at the nearest café, with a couple of pounds and admonitions not to tell their parents. So far David had proved his worth by not telling them but Tony still didn't like parting with his cash.

"Yeah, I suppose."

"You really need to be more understanding of your brother, Tony. He's not like you, he's shy and doesn't make friends easily."

"But Ma!" Tony could feel himself being sucked into the age-old argument in spite of himself. "He's such a loser."

"He's your flesh and blood!"

"I don't get that. He's such a freak."

"If you carry on this way you'll find yourself grounded young man," his father's voice said from behind him. "You show your family some respect. I expect you to be home by six sharp to welcome David home."

Tony stared at his father in dismay. This day was becoming worse and worse. "But Dad, we were ..."

"Do as I say, son. No argument. Now let's have some breakfast."

Tony sat through the meal in sullen silence. He really hated people telling him what to do, especially when it came to his brother. A horn sounded outside and his father quickly kissed his wife on the cheek and ruffled Tony's hair before heading out the door.

"See you all later," he shouted behind him. Tony ran to the window to see the car his father had been allocated by his new company. A bright green Ford sat in the driveway with paint peeling down one side and a dent in the left passenger-side door. The burr in Tony's chest grew larger. It broke a hidden piece of his heart to see what his Dad had come to.

His father waved cheerfully from the front seat as Windsor carefully eased the car into the road and drove off.

"Come finish your breakfast, Tony. It's almost time for school."

"I'm not hungry anymore. I think I'll head on straight."

Laura looked at her son with concern. There was definitely something going on in his head and she was afraid that he was far more astute than either she or her husband had credited him. She knew that Frank was struggling with the change in his life and she'd hoped that their sons hadn't noticed it. Maybe it's something else, she thought, maybe he's just worried about school or girls.

Girls! That's it, she decided with relief. It must be a girl. She looked down at his earnest face with a smile.

"Well here's your lunch box then ... and you go and have a good day."

"Thanks Ma," Tony kissed her on the cheek and rushed out the door. It was time to face the Agnee gang for once and for all.

He ran down First Avenue to the junction of Main where he met Andrew Wiseman, one of his best mates. Andrew was already there waiting for him, a total bookworm and the main reason Tony was still passing school.

"Hey Tone, how you doing?"

"Fine."

"Did you finish your Maths assignment?"

"We had an assignment?" Tony stared at Andrew in horror. A vague memory surfaced of Mrs Fishton giving them a stern reminder that it was due today.

"Oh shit, that assignment!"

Andrew sighed. Tony would never get this right. "Yeah, that assignment. Never mind, we can do it in tea—you can copy mine."

"Thanks Ands. You really are a rescue."

"There is a price though."

Tony dug into his bag and pulled out two of the remaining cherry pops. "Will these do?"

"Hey, where'd you get these? I thought you'd finished your pocket money for the week?"

"Long story, will they do?"

"Definitely."

The two boys started walking along Main towards the school. It wasn't a long walk, not quite a mile.

"Which route we going to take today, Tony?"

"I reckon we go straight," Tony forced down the lump in his throat. Going the easiest way to school was also the route that guaranteed they would bump into the Agnee gang.

"No way! Do you have a death wish? I reckon we go via Park and along the river."

"Today, I'm going straight. You can come with me or you can meet me at school."

Andrew stopped dead in his tracks. "What's going on? Janna gave me a rundown of what happened yesterday. You know these guys are out to get you."

Tony looked his friend straight in the eye, "I spoke to my Uncle Mick last night and he told me what I had to do to get rid of this problem and today I'm gonna do it."

"Oh, excellent, your uncle's waiting for us then? Well that's a different story." Tony realized he had to come clean with his friend.

"No, he isn't."

Andrew couldn't contain his horror. "You mean no cavalry, no miracle muscle, nothing? How do you suppose you're going to survive this?"

"I have to do what he said. I have to," Tony stood firm. He'd made his decision as to what kind of man he was and he wanted to be one that could look his uncle in the eye.

Andrew pondered the situation. He didn't want to leave his friend to handle the gang on his own but he didn't want to end up a bloodstained smudge on the sidewalk either. He was scared and Tony could see it.

"Listen, Ands, you go the back route. This is something I have to do on my own anyway."

This seemed to settle it for Andrew. "No. I'll come with you," he said and he started walking firmly down the road. Tony almost had to run to catch up with him.

"You're sure?"

"Just shut up and walk. I hope to all things mighty that your uncle knows what he's talking about."

"Me too." Tony grinned at Andrew.

"What did he tell you do, if you don't mind me asking? Did he give you special powers or something?'

"Yeah, the power of super-muscles!"

"Or super-stupidity!" retorted Andrew.

"He'd have given you super-reading eyes, geek!"

"Super-geek!"

"I'll give you super-geek," Tony growled mock ferociously, as he pretended to pounce on Andrew. The two of them were laughing so hard that they failed to hear the heavy tread of footsteps around them, or the faint sniggering of the bullies.

"What are you two fags doing now?" sneered Agnee's voice from behind them. Tony nearly jumped out of his skin he got such a fright and Andrew let out a yelp. They both turned around, pale-faced.

"Are the pretty boys fighting to see who gets to wear the dress first?" Agnee waved a pink, frilly frock at the two of them as his buddies sniggered, nastily, behind. Tony stared at the dress in horror—Agnee was really going to force him to wear it. Then his uncle's words came back to him with a force he'd never before experienced and the knot of terror in his stomach disappeared. It was replaced with anger, a powerful, solid rock of anger. He raised his head and looked Agnee in the eye.

"You want a piece of me? Huh? Agnee?" Tony felt indescribably powerful, simply by confronting the bully who had made his life a misery for so long. It was definitely time to take something back.

Agnee was taken aback. This was the first time anyone had ever dared to talk back to him, much less challenge him in any way. He glared at Tony through his piggy eyes as his brain fumbled for a response.

"Well?" Tony stepped forward, into Agnee's personal space, "Do you? Come on, hit me!"

This was something that Agnee understood all too well, so he curled his arm back and let fly with a blow aimed at Tony's nose. Tony watched the meaty arm come for him, as if through treacle, and reacted—he stepped forward, ducked under the punch and kicked Agnee in the crotch as hard as he possibly could. Every moment of torture and frustration he'd ever experienced was poured into that kick. He gave it all he had. Agnee fell like a stone. The surrounding goons stared at their leader in dismay—a wailing wreck on the ground, with both hands wrapped over his groin in protective agony. Agnee let out a scream and all hell broke loose. The double-Ts turned tail and ran as fast as their legs could carry them; they didn't even turn around to see if anyone followed.

Tony stood over his rocking body and grabbed Agnee's chin.

"Don't ever come near me again, is that clear?"

"I'll leave you alone Tony, I promise."

The pitiful whimper that ended the sentence drove home to Tony that this was truly it. He would never have to worry about being bullied by this gang again. He dropped Agnee's head, picked up his knapsack and turned to see if Andrew was alright.

His friend was frozen, in the same pose he'd been in since the fracas began, with a look of utter shock on his face.

"You okay?"

"You kicked him in the balls, you did it Tony, you did it!"

The news of Tony's heroism spread through the school like wildfire. He spent the day being patted on the back, cheered and thanked.

"It hasn't turned out to be such a bad day after all," he commented to Janna, as they sat having lunch on the field.

"Were you scared this morning?"

"Definitely," Tony felt there was no shame in admitting this—he'd won and was feeling every inch the hero.

"I can't believe that this is what your uncle told you to do! It's so ... so ... brutish!"

Tony gave her an exasperated look, "He was right wasn't he?"

"Yeah, he was. But that doesn't mean I approve of it."

"Hey guys," a soft voice said behind them.

"Hey, Colleen," they chorused, shifting up on the stone wall to give her some room. A pudgy little girl clambered up beside them, her long blonde hair flopping in her eyes. "Ands is on his way and Ian is doing detention. Something about throwing chalk at Mrs Winthrop."

"Again? He seems to love getting into the same kind of trouble," Janna sighed. "Where's Cal?"

"He's on his way," mumbled Janna as she bit into her sandwich. "He's always late."

"Well I have some big news and I can't wait anymore."

"What?" Tony asked.

"My parents are going away and my cousin, Nancy, is coming to look after my brother and me. You remember Nancy, don't you?"

"Yes!" Tony shot his arms up in the air. The day could not get better. Colleen's cousin Nancy was only eighteen and she let them get up to all sorts of mischief.

"When?"

"Next weekend. It's perfect! You guys can come stay for the weekend and we can play spin-the-bottle." Colleen was determined to inveigle Calvin into any compromising position she could.

Janna laughed at her expression, "Yes, we can."

Just then Andrew and Calvin came up and the five of them sat on the wall laughing and talking about the weekend ahead and the wonders of beating the Agnee gang.

Chapter Four

Seven years later.

Tony lay on his bed staring up at the ceiling. In three months' time he was going to be writing his final exams and he knew that he had NO hope of passing. Until now he'd got by with luck and cheating. Mostly cheating. Andrew Wiseman had practically dragged him through school so far, by allowing him to copy his work and helping him hide notes about his person during exams, but the final year exams were different. Very different. This time he was going to have to study and, because he'd done very little so far, it meant that there was no way he was going to pass. He was also determined not to stay back another year at school. Ten years was quite enough for him thank you very much. So he lay on his bed with his hands behind his head thinking up one scheme after another and dismissing each one for having one major failing or another. His ceiling began to take on another worldly quality, as the pressed ceiling pattern of rectangular squares wrapped around each other and twisted and curled under the intensity of his stare.

He sat up and shook his head; sitting around moping wasn't going to get him anywhere. It was time to call in the gang. Maybe all their minds working together could come up with something useful. After pulling on some clothes he walked the two or so blocks down the road to Janna's place and knocked on the door.

An attractive older woman with strong features answered the door. "Tony," she said, not without a little tension in her voice. Mrs Maitland wasn't entirely happy about her daughter's association with the Meyer's boy. To her he reeked of trouble.

"Good afternoon, Mrs Maitland. How are you?"

"I'm well. I gather you're here to visit Janna?" She couldn't fault him on his manners. It was a constant source of annoyance.

"If that's alright?"

"She's out in the garden with Calvin and Colleen."

Tony grinned. It was perfect—pretty much everyone was here already.

"Thanks," he said, as he stepped past her into the cool interior of the home. Janna's home reminded him of candy; her mother seemed to have an endless passion for yellow and pink so every room was filled with paints, porcelains and flowers of those colours. Spending too long in this house tended to give him a headache. He practically ran through the lounge into the back garden but, as he reached the door, her paused. Janna sat on a deck chair in the sun, her hair shone and her face glowed. She was laughing at something Colleen had said and her whole face was alight with happiness. He wished he could freeze this moment in time. One day, he vowed. One day I am going to marry this girl.

"Hey," he said, stepping out of the shade.

Three pairs of eyes lit up. "Hey Tony," they chorused. "Come have a seat."

"Do you want something to drink?" asked Janna, giving him a sweet little smile.

"Absolutely, what's on offer?"

"Lemonade or iced tea."

"Mmm, iced tea, please." He settled himself on the grass beside Colleen and gave her a lascivious wink. Last Friday's spin-the-bottle session, a game that they never seemed to tire of, had been a pretty interesting one with her. She'd let his wandering hands wander a little further than usual, plus hinted at the chance of something more. At the time he'd almost considered it but thoughts of Janna had soon put that from his mind. He wondered what had happened to Calvin. In the last seven years their group hadn't changed much, with the exception of occasional new boyfriends and girlfriends adopted by the various members, nor had the affections of Colleen for Calvin or Tony for Janna. Recently, it had looked as if Calvin was finally starting to notice Colleen's charms but, maybe, it was too late for her. Who knew? Tony shrugged to himself—women were fickle at the best of times. In spite of his obvious flirtations with Janna she'd never allowed him more than a few secretive kisses. She dated plenty of other boys, that was for sure, but they never lasted more than a month or two and then she was right back with him. Tony didn't begrudge her this. In fact he rather liked the arrangement.

" … do you think, Tony?" Colleen's voice interrupted his thoughts.

"Sorry? I wasn't listening," he laughed. "Lost in my thoughts there."

"Obviously. Well, we were debating the onset of exams."

"Oh. That," Tony sighed. "That's why I was looking for you actually. I need a foolproof plan to pass, because there is no way I'm staying back here."

"I told you to stop relying on Andy," Janna needled him as she came back with his drink, "If you'd listened you wouldn't be in this position."

"Well I am, so I need to figure out a rescue plan … fast."

"Why don't you steal the exam papers?" laughed Colleen. "That'll ensure you pass alright."

They all started laughing, except Tony. Of course! It was so simple he hadn't even thought of it. He knew exactly where they were hidden and with careful planning it would be so easy for him to steal them. He stood, "I'll see you guys later, I have some planning to do."

The other three stopped laughing and stared at him.

"I was joking, Tony," said Colleen nervously.

"I know but I think it could work."

"You can't be serious," gasped Janna, "If you get caught ..."

"IF I get caught and I won't. Not if I plan this properly."

"There must be another way, surely," Janna insisted.

"It's easy enough," said Calvin, looking thoughtfully at Tony, "We could do it."

"And we can make some money in the process."

"What!" shouted Janna and Colleen in unison, both utterly horrified.

"Well, if we sell the papers to every person in final year we could make a killing. We could even go to other schools and sell them there too."

"I won't be a part of this," Janna said firmly. "No way. You shouldn't even be considering it at all. If you get caught you'll lose everything. I've worked too hard to throw it away on something like this."

Tony looked at Janna tenderly. "I would never ask this of you, Janna. If I do it then I'll do it myself."

"No, not by yourself. I'm in," said Calvin. "I'm looking at a miserable pass myself and I still want to go to college."

"Ands'll do it too, I reckon. Let's go get him and find out." Calvin and Tony waved a brisk farewell to the shell-shocked girls and left to find Andrew. They were energized by their idea. Not only would it mean a brilliant final pass but they'd make some holiday money too. They were full of ideas as they walked, half-ran to Andrew's house, about how much they would charge the other students and what they would spend the money on.

"Hey!" Tony said breathlessly as Andrew opened the door, "We've had a brainwave." Andrew eyed them both suspiciously.

"Right, you'd better come in then."

The moment Andy shut the door to his room behind them Tony started talking. "We've figured out how I'm going to pass my exams!"

"How?"

"We're going to steal the papers!"

"You're joking!"

"Not a chance. Not only that, we're going to sell them to all the other students in final year and not just at our school either."

Andrew was remarkably unperturbed by these revelations, after all he'd been Tony's friend for several years. "When?"

"Well, the papers will be sent through sometime next month, so all we have to do is figure out how we're going to do it and then simply go for it once they're here."

"Hmmm," Andrew mused, "They keep the papers locked in the school records' room until the exams and it's pretty easy to slip in through the windows."

"But they keep the windows covered in brown paper," interrupted Calvin. "If it's torn or moved then they'll know someone's been inside."

"Oh please! That's easy to fix. All we need is some brown paper and some tape and we can cover it up, no problem," scoffed Tony.

"Yeah, but how are you going to paper the windows up from the outside?" asked Calvin. "Outside?"

"Well you're going to have to get out of the room, remember?"

"No man, once I'm inside all I have to do is go out through the door. It's one of those slip locks that can be opened from the inside."

"Of course! Shit, I'm such an idiot."

"Nah, you made a good point," said Andrew. "Well, we have to figure out a way to get inside the school. What's the plan?"

"Okay, you guys know I can climb pretty much anything, right?"

"Right," they replied.

"So I'll climb up the big drainpipe outside the recreation room wall. Once I'm in there I can go through the school to the offices. Then I'll need something to shimmy open the window. Any ideas?"

"You could use some wire, slip it underneath the one edge and with a bit of fiddling you should be able to get the hook loose."

"Perfect, so I'll jimmy the window, climb inside, steal one set of papers from each subject, go out through the main door after papering up the window and then meet you guys outside the rec-room door. Then we'll have to copy all the papers that night and I'll simply go through all the open doors, replace the papers and get out. Nobody will know!"

"Copy the papers?"

"Well, we can't keep them, can we? We'll have to write down all the questions in one go."

"That's going to be a killer," said Andrew, "We're going to need help."

"Maybe Ian will help us out."

"And the girls," said Calvin.

"They said they didn't want anything to do with this."

"Janna said she didn't, but maybe she won't mind if it's just copying down stuff," said Calvin.

"That's true," Tony nodded approvingly. "Maybe she won't."

"Are you really going to sell them?"

"Oh definitely. That's going to require some thought, so I'll let you know what plan I've cooked up as soon as I've sorted it out. I may just go to the head of each class and ask them to do it. They can take a commission and they'll make sure nobody tells, otherwise they'll be in trouble too."

"Good thinking there," said Andrew, "What are we going to charge?"

"I'm thinking five pounds a paper. You'll all get a percentage, but I'm going to take the biggest cut because I'll be the front man on the whole deal. Fair?"

"Sounds fair to me," said Andrew, "Cal?"

"Me too. Sounds fine."

The boys put their heads together and sorted out most of the finer details that afternoon. Over the next few weeks they walked all around the school and surreptitiously checked out the offices and their escape routes. By the time the papers were delivered they had a solid plan in place and were itching to put it into action. The whole gang was involved, including Janna, who felt that a night of copying didn't make her feel quite as bad as the actual act of stealing. Tony led the entire process, of course, and made sure that all the conspirators knew their roles perfectly. When it came to the night that they were to make their move everyone was more excited than scared.

Tony was wearing as much black as he could find, which wasn't much since it wasn't his favourite colour, but at least he wasn't too colourful in the night light. He met up with Ian, Calvin and Andy at the corner of the street by the school. The other three were nervously pacing up and down when he arrived.

"Tony!" Andrew couldn't keep the relief out of his voice, "You're here!"

"Of course I'm here," he said, amused at Andy's reaction, "Where'd you think I'd be? Swimming?"

"Oh, ha ha! You're late."

"Yeah, sorry about that. I had to give David the slip. You know how he is."

"Oh, right. Did you get rid of him? You sure?" Ian peered out into the shadows suspiciously. Tony's brother was like a limpet mine once he became attached to an idea and Ian had no idea how they were going to explain their going for a walk with brown paper, ropes and wire.

"I'm sure," said Tony impatiently, "Come on, let's go."

They carefully climbed the fence to the rugby field and made their way to the back of the school, using all the patches of darkness around them. It would have taken a very keen eye to spot them as they ran.

"We're here," said Tony as he unravelled the rope around his neck. "I'm going to climb up the side here and tie the rope in the middle, just in case. You guys keep an eye out for anyone. The moment I'm inside, take off the rope, go round to the office area and wait for me. Okay?"

"Okay, Tony."

"Be careful, buddy," whispered Andy, as Tony grabbed hold of the pipe and started to pull himself up.

"Surely." Tony gave him a cocky grin and thumbs-up before he turned and faced his task in earnest. It didn't take him long to scale the side of the building and slip in through the window to the gymnasium.

He jumped down to the floor and dusted his hands in satisfaction. That went well, he thought. Very well indeed.

He quickly made his way through the school to the offices and came up to the brown-papered window, which held his salvation. It was a matter of moments for him to wriggle the wire through the bottom of the window and flip up the hook that held it in place. Soon he was inside the room. Several rows of metal cabinets lay before him in the darkness. He smiled. The papers. Here at last was his big chance. All those months of planning and here he was. Tony couldn't resist a quiet whoop of delight.

Again, it was really easy for him to replace the damaged paper on the window and return things to normal. He studied his work critically. No difference from the original at all. "Perhaps I've missed my calling," he mused. "It's perfect."

He opened the first two cabinets and found them full of school records and student information. For a moment he was tempted to see what his teachers had to say about him and his friends. Perhaps even that idiot Simon Parker, who was always wandering around with his nose either in a book, or in the air. It would be fabulous to sidle up to him at lunch break and make a choice remark to shake that annoying pomposity. Then he shook himself—time was of the essence. He found what he needed in the last two cabinets at the end of the row and carefully took one paper from each set. Then he picked up all his tools, did a final check to make sure that nothing was left behind which could give him away, and then he left.

The guys were waiting for him outside the main office door and the three of them ran straight to Janna's house where the girls were waiting to help them copy everything down.

Tony rang the bell and Janna's mother answered. For a moment Tony's heart leapt into his throat. Her parents were supposed to be going out for the evening. Had Janna told them what they were doing? How had they found out?

"Ah, you're here," said Mrs Maitland. "We're about to leave. We'll see you children later."

Tony breathed an inaudible sigh of relief. All was still on track. The boys tramped into the lounge where a pale-faced Janna was sitting and making small talk with her father and Colleen.

"Ah, right. You're here. Well, we had better be off then," said Mr Maitland with evident relief.

Clearly chatting to teenage girls wasn't his idea of entertainment. Janna's relief was palpable and Tony gave her a quick wink while surreptitiously patting his backpack. Her eyes widened and she practically chased her parents out the house.

"Come! Upstairs, quickly!" she urged, once the coast was clear.

Her entire room had been prepared for the event. Pens and paper sat in five neat piles on the floor. Tony pulled the papers out of his bag and handed them around.

"Let's get cracking," he said. "We haven't got much time and I need to get them back before daylight."

"Let's do it!" shouted Colleen. They sat in huddles on the floor, writing furiously and muttering to themselves. It took them the entire night to finish copying the exam papers, interrupted only by Janna bringing in more coffee and the occasional gasp of 'I know this!' or 'That's a terrible question!'

The first glints of false dawn were rising on the morning sky when they finished and Tony was a mess of screaming nerves. If they got caught or if anyone even remotely suspected foul play then this would have all been for nothing. He had to get back to the school and replace everything at once.

It was then that they had the biggest scare, which could have changed everything.

The envelopes had been sealed with red wax, which the boys had carefully steamed, lifting the seals with a craft knife. Tony put the papers back in the envelopes and began to paste the flaps down with Lapagers glue. He stopped cold; the steam had bleached the red wax. As his hand froze in mid air and his stomach churned, a drop of glue splashed down and landed with a plop on the seal, turning it red. It was only then that Tony realized he had stopped breathing completely. As he sucked air in through his teeth, he started to drop glue on to each seal.

"Hell, that was a close one," breathed Colleen.

Tony carefully placed the envelopes in his bag, grabbed Andrew's bike and raced off to the school. He barely made it in time. Just as he closed the door to the office behind him he heard voices in the corridor ahead. He looked wildly to his left and right. Where was he going to hide? There was no way he could explain his presence at the school so early.

"I know what you mean, Harriet," said Principal Wilder. "It has definitely been a very dry spring."

"I do hope it's not another drought, Frank. We've already had two very tough years."

"I'm sure it will be fine …"

Their voices walked past Tony so closely that he believed he could reach out and touch them. He waited in his hiding place beneath the secretary's desk until he was sure they were out of sight and then he got out of there as fast as he could. In spite of his lack of sleep and cramping right hand Tony had had one of the most exhilarating days of his life. Between the fear of someone discovering their secret and elation at his trickery, he bounced through the day.

That night Tony and the gang got together to talk about the upcoming exams and what to do about the papers they had stolen. As Tony walked to Janna's place he went over his new plan once more before telling the others. It was a brilliant idea which had come to him while he had been daydreaming in Maths class, but he had to have the complete agreement of all his friends before he implemented it. It was a lovely evening, the heat of the day had mellowed into a gentle warmth and a jasmine-scented spring breeze fluffed the ends of his hair as he rang Janna's doorbell.

"Good evening, Tony," said Janna's mother as she opened the door. "I see the whole bunch of you have gathered tonight." She said this with a warm smile as she stepped aside so he could enter. "Everyone is outside on the patio. Help yourself to some lemonade on the way."

Tony smiled back, "Thank you, Mrs Maitland. I will."

He walked straight into the kitchen and poured himself some juice before joining the others. He was a little nervous about what he was about to suggest to the group, mainly because it was something he really wanted.

"Hi guys," he grinned as he stepped out onto the patio. "How's things?"

"Great!" laughed Calvin. "We're busy celebrating our crime of the century."

"Shhh, Calvin!" exclaimed Colleen. "Not so loud; we don't want Janna's parents to hear."

"I wasn't speaking that loudly," he retorted. "Relax."

"I'll relax when we know for sure that nobody finds out. If this gets out we're ruined!" Colleen's voice held a trace of panic and her face reddened. Janna reached out and took her friend's hand reassuringly.

"Oh just …" snapped Calvin, but Janna interrupted, "No, she's right Calvin. This is a big deal and I'm worried that we've got carried away with the whole excitement of it without thinking things through."

Tony sighed inwardly. The way things were going right now there was no way that anyone would agree to his new plan, so he sat quietly and waited for everyone to bring their fears out into the open. Often fears seem smaller when they have been released.

"I disagree," said Andrew. "We were very careful and nobody has said a thing. Surely they would have noticed by now if anything was wrong?"

"I'm not so sure," replied Janna. "The exams only start next week, so maybe nobody has even gone into that office today."

"Now that can't be true," said Calvin, "All sorts of records are kept in there—even school files—they had to have been there already and if they'd noticed anything then we would know about it by now."

"Actually I think he may be right," Colleen said suddenly and unexpectedly. " Johnny Henkins was called into the principal's office today and the principal always has our files out when he talks to us."

"Really? Johnny Henkins? What did he do?" asked Tony, curious.

"Never mind that!" snapped Calvin. "The important thing is that nobody has the faintest clue of what we did last night. We're free and clear."

'Tony?" Janna tilted her head as she looked at him, her dark eyes piercing. "What do you think?" Tony was silent for a moment before replying, "I think that we've got away with it so far."

"So far?" Andrew's voice was nervous, "What do you mean 'so far'?"

"I mean that we still have to be careful and we obviously can't do that well in the exams either—that alone would be suspicious."

"Well that's blindingly obvious," sneered Calvin. "What else?"

"Don't talk about it. Ever. To anyone—not even each other."

"That's crazy," said Janna. "We're talking about it now for goodness sake."

"Unless we are all together I mean," replied Tony. "That way we prevent anyone from overhearing us, or one of us letting it slip. It is so important that nobody can ever link this to any of us. Especially if we do one more thing."

"What one more thing?"

"What are you talking about?"

"Hey!"

Tony waited for the panic to die down before raising his hand placatingly. "Wait, guys, hear me out first."

"It was your crazy idea that got us here in the first place!" Calvin shouted. "And now you want us to do even more? What could you possibly have in mind?"

Tony smiled, "What I have in mind will sort out your financial problems in a second and it won't get us into any trouble at all. Not if we're careful."

"Go ahead, I'm listening," said Andrew who was curious, in spite of himself.

"Me too," said Colleen, surprising everyone.

"Well, why don't we sell these papers to every single school in the area?"

"What!"

Again everyone's voices were raised in debate as Tony just sat and watched with a smug smirk on his face until Mr Maitland came out onto the patio.

"What's going on out here?" he demanded. "Are you kids having a fight?"

Everyone immediately fell silent, unable to meet Janna's father's eyes. Tony took stock of the situation and intervened.

"Not at all, Mr Maitland," he said calmly. "We were just debating something we learnt in Biology today. Most of us have differing opinions."

"Oh," Mr Maitland said, surveying the group with a stern eye. "Well, keep it down, I'm not in the mood for shouting while I'm trying to relax after work."

"Sorry sir," said Tony and was followed by a chorus of subdued 'Sorry sir' as Mr Maitland turned and left the room.

Tony's cool composure in handling what could have been a nasty situation caused everyone in the group look at him in a different light. He clearly wasn't fazed by what was going on and even the unnerving arrival of Janna's father hadn't broken that. Tony could sense immediately that the mood of the group was turning towards him and he seized his opportunity with both hands.

"Think about it!" he said. "We could charge everyone a set rate per paper and we could insist that every single class member be involved before we commit to handing any copies over. That way, everyone is equally guilty and nobody will turn anyone in."

"But, what if the person we approach doesn't buy into this and goes straight to his teacher or principal?" asked Janna.

Tony looked at her with respect. She really was a wonderfully smart young woman. "Now that is the best part. We only approach the class captains from each school and when we do we make sure that we don't give anything away up front.

"Think about it, if we hint at what we have then they may take the bait and, once we have them hooked, we'll have enough hold over them to get them into as much trouble as they would us."

"I think you should definitely handle the negotiations then," said Andrew with a sigh. "I have no idea on how to be that subtle."

"Great, I will, but I'll need your help in finding out who all the different class captains are and how to get to meet them."

"I can do that," said Colleen, "I like doing that kind of thing."

"I'll help," said Janna.

"Wait!" exclaimed Calvin. "We haven't even thought through the basics yet."

"Like what?" asked Tony

"Like how much we're going to charge and who's going to be spending all their valuable studying time copying down the papers."

"You don't need to study, you dolt," sneered Tony. "You have the papers already remember?" Tony let out an exasperated sigh.

"I'm not going to use the papers."

"What?"

"You heard me, I am not going to use those papers to study for my exams."

"Why on earth not?"

"Yes, Cal, why not?" asked Colleen.

"Because I want to pass on my own merit and I want to know that I did so fairly, that's all."

"That's fair enough," said Andrew. "I'm probably going to do the same thing."

"Well you're both smart enough to do that," said Tony, "but I'm not. I'll use the papers to pass and I'll do all the copying for the papers we're going to sell. Better?" He inclined his head towards Calvin.

"That's fine, but please don't ask me to help because I really don't want to cheat."

"No problem. Why don't you help Colleen and Janna then?"

"Actually I was thinking that Andrew and I could help you."

"How?"

"I'm pretty good at persuasion myself. I think I can help you bring a few class captains under our spell."

Tony was impressed. His initial reaction to Calvin's earlier decision had been one of derision but this was both an unexpected and welcome idea.

"That's a great idea. You're in."

"What are we going to charge people for this?" asked Janna, "It can't be too expensive but it also can't be too cheap."

"I was thinking about five pounds, actually," said Tony. "It isn't a lot in the grand scheme of things, but it certainly isn't a pittance."

"That's perfect!" said Colleen. "It's cheap enough to let everyone on board but expensive enough to show that we mean business. Great plan Tony!"

Colleen winked at Tony as he turned to answer another question from Calvin and he realized that her affections had transferred to him. Excellent, he thought, there might be a much warmer and softer end to my week than I had anticipated.

A few weeks later, Tony and the gang met up at their favourite spot by the river to catch up on the news of their respective plans. Tony, Calvin and Andrew had managed to sell the papers to five of the schools in the area. They had made over five thousand pounds and were on a high that was difficult to break. Tony was bouncing all over the place with excitement—he couldn't believe that his simple idea had borne such amazing fruit. Now he could go away for a few months after school on a well-earned holiday and he could buy himself a car. Life was beautiful.

"... to be obvious," Andrew was saying to an astonished Colleen and Janna. Obviously he'd just told them about their cash haul and they were too stunned to make any comment.

"This is unbelievable," Janna managed eventually, "Five thousand pounds? I mean, that's incredible."

"Indeed it is," said Tony. "You'll all be getting about six hundred and fifty pounds each and I'm keeping the rest."

"What!" shouted Calvin, closely followed by Andrew. "How come you get to keep so much?

"I'll tell you why," said Tony as he stepped forward directly into Calvin's space. "It's because I am the one who came up with all these ideas. I am the one who spent the last three weeks copying paper after paper and I am the one whose hands are the dirtiest and I am the one most likely to get caught."

"But ..."

"What? You have a problem with this?" Tony snarled, showing his true amoral nature to his friend for the first time. "Why don't you go and tell your mommy. No? Why not daddy then? Oh, wait, then you'd have to explain how you know so much and where the money came from."

Tony gave Calvin a little push. "I don't think so. Surely even you can respect the fact that I did most of the work?"

"He's right, Cal," said Colleen. "This was all his idea and we wouldn't even have this money if it wasn't for him. I say it's fair."

"Me too," said Janna, and Andrew nodded at Tony, holding his eye.

Calvin looked around and then nodded, "Sure, right," he said. Then he shook himself and stepped closer to Tony with his hand outstretched, "Sorry man, I didn't think."

Tony magnanimously took his hand and shook it—he could afford to be magnanimous since he had now won his own way. Inwardly he smirked; friends were good and well but ultimately, it was only Andrew and Janna who really meant anything to him. After all, it was Andrew who'd helped him through school year after year and who'd unfailingly given of his time to make sure that his mate would pass. Andrew was also getting extra cash—a fact Calvin didn't need to know.

"Well I'm off," he said. "I've gotta be at home early today for supper. It's David's birthday today."

"Oh yes!" exclaimed Janna. "I forgot. How is he doing?'

"Fine, I suppose."

"Honestly Tony, you shouldn't be so hard on your brother," said Colleen. "Family is important."

"Yeah. Sure," Tony muttered as he took his leave. He grabbed his pack from the where he'd left it on the wall and shrugged into his windbreaker. Winter was clearly on its way and the wind had a sharp bite to it.

"Cheers guys," he called as he made his way up the embankment. As he walked, he pondered his fate. It was almost time for him to leave the confines of school and to finally get out into the world and do things that really appealed to him. No more rules and regulations, no more parents telling him what to do. Finally he could spread those wings he supposedly had and fly off to experience the multitude of opportunities that the world presented.

It was totally excellent, there but was one crisis still to overcome.

In January, Tony, with his matric in the bag, had obtained a position with a clothing store where the headmaster had phoned several weeks later, wanting a chat with Tony before work one morning.

The police met him at the headmaster's office, claiming to have a witness to the theft of the matric papers. Tony knew that it had to be the one person who had not bought the papers from him, the only one out of about a thousand kids who had failed his exams—it seems there is always one rat. Charlie Schwartz didn't have the cash to pay for the papers and as per the agreement with the prefects, he couldn't copy from any of the other kids who, quite frankly, had paid good money for their guaranteed pass. Tony was pretty sure it was he who had ratted on them, but, that was actually good news, because he was very sure that Charlie had not actually witnessed their stealing the papers.

Adrenaline pumped through Tony's body as he used every ounce of willpower he had to hold the detectives' piercing gaze.

Tony knew it wasn't going to be a friendly encounter and was prepared for the men in blue. But still, he wasn't sure his stomach was up to it as he stared back.

"If you have witnesses then bring them forward, otherwise you're wasting my time." He turned on his heel, hands in pockets to stop them shaking and walked out the door.

He never heard from them again and later he'd had a 'little chat' with Charlie.

Charlie knew it wasn't worth his life to blab again.

Q: So, that's how you made your first big money. What did you spend it on?

A. *Tony sits back and laughs.* Well, I was too scared to spend a penny. I stashed the lot in my mother's garage, so apart from buying a car, I had most of it when I moved to Rhodesia.

Chapter
Five

Tony's car was a Citroën. It came second-hand from an uncle who was in the motor trade. It was black with grey upholstery. It took Tony to and from his job with a clothing wholesaler, where he worked in dispatch. His boss gave him a tank of petrol a week.

At night Tony and his friends went to the clubs in Hillbrow. They picked up girls and danced and drank beer. They took the girls joyriding down Harrow Road then went to the Wilds to kiss and cuddle in the park-like gardens. The tank of petrol didn't last very long.

"Come on, guys, I'm fed up paying for petrol all the time. What about some contributions?"

"We haven't got money, Tony."

"You've got money for beer and girls, Merv."

"It's not enough, Tony. But I'm getting my first cheque next week. I'll help out then."

"I've got an idea, Tony. I'll bring some tools from the garage tomorrow and we'll drain a few tanks."

"About time your dad taught you something useful, Trevor."

"Yeah, Trevor, you've been at the garage for months now."

"I've had to teach myself. He only let's me do oil changes …
apprentice stuff. But I watch the mechanics."

It was much more fun stealing petrol than paying for it. They
chose their cars with care. Older cars parked in dark side streets. Cars
in small parking lots behind noisy clubs. One night they picked a
small sedan parked on the forecourt of a garage. It squatted between
the other vehicles like a shy girl at a tea party. The cars on either
side gave good cover. Trevor lay under the car undoing the drainage
nut on the fuel tank. Tony sprawled alongside him, holding the old
oilcan. The petrol started to leak from the half-opened nut. Now
you had to be clever. If you opened the nut too far it would explode
out of its hole, propelled by the force of petrol. If you didn't open it
far enough the petrol would drip out too slowly. Trevor got it just
right and the oilcan filled in seconds. He tightened the nut while he
waited for Tony to pass the can to Mervin. Mervin took the can to the
Citroën and he and Sid poured the petrol into the tank. They started
to fill the can for the third time when heavy footsteps and loud
yelling shattered the quiet night.

"Aikona, aikona. Wat doen jy? Hey, totsis!"

"Shit, let's go, let's go."

Tony and Trevor were out from under the car. The Citroën's
engine was already racing and they ran for the doors. The big black
man raised his knobkerrie. Tony ducked, bobbed sideways and
the bulbous end of the ugly weapon hit the pavement. They threw
themselves through the open doors and the Citroën sped away down
the road. Sid watched the guard in the rearview mirror who was still
shouting and gesticulating wildly as they turned the corner.

"Jesus Christ, Sid, you were meant to be on the lookout."

"He must have been sleeping behind the pumps. It was like he
appeared from nowhere."

"You're lucky he missed you, Tony. You'd be dead," said Mervin.

Chapter 5

"He knows how to handle that thing. We'll stay away from this area in future."

"Shit, we left all the tools."

"And the petrol cap was on top of the car."

"Just look out for another Citroën. We've got to have a petrol cap," said Tony.

The police were at Prinsloo's Service Station the next morning.

"Mr Prinsloo, one of your boys is stealing petrol. He was stupid enough to leave his tools behind and they're all marked with this garage's name."

"I'll get the head mechanic to call the staff. If the culprit doesn't own up, take them all down to the station," replied Mr Prinsloo.

The mechanics stood, scowling with arms crossed, in the office. The smell of sweat, old engine oil and grease competed with the aroma of coffee and Constable Coetzee's mints. Trevor stood with his back to the wall. He could see the tools lying on his father's desk and moved to the window. The head mechanic placed his backside on the sill and stretched his legs out in front of him. Trevor looked at the huge steel-tipped boots, followed the blue-overalled legs up to the massive arms crossed over the wide chest. A home-done tattoo scarred the man's forearm. He looked at the man's face, dark-bearded, dark-eyed. The crewcut accentuated a square, bony head. The man turned his head toward Trevor and held him in an unblinking gaze. Trevor felt the blood rise in his neck, burning his ears. He tore his eyes away, stared at the floor.

"Right, everyone's here now, so let's get on. Whose are these tools?"

Trevor put his hands to the wall and pushed himself into the circle of men. He was more afraid of the mechanic than of his father's wrath.

"They're mine, Dad."

He saw his father's face drop; the flesh became soft on the cheekbones, the eyes dull. Constable Coetzee stepped up beside him and took out his notebook.

"Have you been stealing petrol?"

"I'm sorry, Dad. It was just some fun."

"Taking things that don't belong to you is not what you do for fun. It's theft, a criminal offence."

"He'll have to come to the station, Mr Prinsloo. Charges have been laid."

"Let my men get back to work, constable. Then maybe you can have some coffee."

"That would be appreciated, Mr Prinsloo."

It was almost five o' clock. Tony was filling his last order. He placed the pair of charcoal trousers in the box, added the invoice and closed the cardboard lid. He pulled the string from the dispenser and tied it tightly round the carton. Checked the label and placed the box next to the other five lined up by the door. They would be loaded in the morning. He heard the door to the administration office open and turned to see Mr Traumann coming in with two policemen. He knew they were coming to see him.

Mr Traumann let him leave five minutes early. He stood at the door, watching Tony drive away in his own car, accompanied by one of the policemen. They followed the police van to the police station. Mervin and Sid were already there. The sergeant directed Tony to wait with them on the hard bench outside the constable's office. They sat close together, leaning forward, heads bent over hands.

"Trevor's got out of this one, then."

"His dad's got influence."

"He's going to testify against us. His dad's made a deal."

"I'm going to lose my job over this, Tony. You can't work in the diamond fields with a criminal record," Mervin said anxiously.

"Well, that's what I've been thinking about, guys. You've both got more to lose than me. Sid'll lose his scholarship and you'll get kicked out of your job, Merv."

"You'll probably also lose your job, Tony."

"I've got money so it doesn't matter. I'm going to carry this one. You've both got to deny any involvement. I'll plead guilty. You guys turn State's evidence."

"I can't let you do that, Tony."

"Why not, Sid? You think you'll get another scholarship? Don't be stupid."

"What if you go to jail?"

"We took a bit of petrol. The worst they'll do is send me to reform school."

Tony stood in front of the mirror. He sprinkled his hands with hair oil and ran his fingers over his scalp. He took up his brush and tamed the brown curls, smoothing the short sides and allowing the longer hair on top to spring up a little. He wiped his hands on a towel then ran his fingers over his chin, feeling the smooth skin, pleased that he'd shaved with such care. He straightened his tie, adjusted the jacket over the collar of his white shirt and picked up his car keys from the dresser. He was wearing his best suit, made for him by an Indian tailor in Fordsburg, so well cut that it gave him height, reduced his bulky shoulders. He left the house through the back door, kissing Mom's cheek on his way out, assuring her he wasn't hungry and that he had to go to work.

He drove to the magistrate's court. He was early and he sat in the car for a while, watching the pedestrians—the black man in beige overalls sweeping the edge of the pavement, the people pushing their way through the doors to the building. He looked at his watch. He had to find Court 15. It was time for him to go. The time had come.

The dark-haired girl at reception gave him directions in Afrikaans. She smiled at him, smoothed her hair and pointed down the long corridor. He thanked her, said he'd see her at lunchtime. She said she ate her lunch under the tree in the park round the corner; Tony said he'd see her there. He found Court 15 and was told to wait on the bench until he was called.

Sid and Mervin arrived a few minutes later. They had been summonsed to give evidence against him. The case against Trevor had been dropped.

They were called into court at eleven o'clock. The magistrate sat at his elevated desk. Tony stood in the dock, looking up at him as the charge was read out. The magistrate laid the charge sheet on the desk, pushed his glasses up his nose and glared at Tony.

"How do you plead, young man?"

"Guilty, your honour."

The judge looked down at the charge sheet.

"You used tools from Prinsloo's Garage. How did you come by these tools?"

"Mr. Prinsloo's son is a friend of mine. He was showing me how to service my car. He left the tools at my house."

"The statement from the witness, Joseph Mlanga, says there were four of you involved."

"He must be mistaken, your honour. *I* was taking the petrol. My friends tried to stop me. I wouldn't listen."

"And now you are in court."

"I'm very sorry, your honour, I've learnt my lesson."

"I'm not going to waste any more time on this. I sentence you to one year, suspended for three years. I do not want to see you in my court ever again."

"Yes, sir."

"As for your friends, they're very lucky young men. They should be in the dock with you. I know you're taking the rap for them. One day they'll have to repay you and I sincerely hope they do."

Q: And did they ever repay you?

A: That's not what mates are about. If the situation had been reversed, I hope they would have done the same for me.

Q: Talking about mates, what happened to all your school mates?

A: We'd drifted apart, they'd all gone off to college and I socialized with appy types.

Chapter
Six

Mr Traumann knew when he had a good employee and decided to overlook Tony's indiscretion. He challenged him with hard work, in the belief that Tony would be too tired to go out at night. Tony worked at the pace set by Mr Traumann and waited for his first cheque. At the end of the month he cashed the twenty-pound cheque at the bank and took the notes home. He spread them on his bed, laid aside the money for his mother and considered the rest. He felt he'd be comfortably off if only he had an extra three pounds.

Mr Traumann was delighted with his decision to keep Tony on and, within three months, promoted him to dispatch manager and increased his salary by ten pounds. Tony was efficient, knew all the products and worked harder than ever. When he received his first cheque in his new position he thought if only he had ten pounds more he'd be satisfied. He would show Mr. Traumann that he deserved those extra ten pounds and he worked to make the dispatch department the most efficient department in the factory. After six months Mr Traumann was so impressed that he promoted Tony to warehouse manager and doubled his salary. Tony was thrilled with his new position and couldn't wait for his big cheque at the end of the month. He rushed to cash it at the bank and spread the money on his bed. He was startled to realize that he still wasn't happy. He thought about how he could earn yet another ten pounds.

He started to talk to the salesmen when they came every week to pick up their orders. They explained how their commission structure worked and Tony realized that there was no limit to their monthly income. He nagged Mr Traumann about going on the road. Mr Traumann eventually agreed to let him try the concessions route. He would visit the general merchandise shops that traded next to the mines. These shops were called concession stores and were generally delegated to Jews. They sold groceries, pharmaceuticals, tinware, chinaware, clothing ranges and household goods. They also acted as post office and bank to the migrant labourers. Where there was a mine there was a concession store and Tony drove the Witwatersrand from Krugersdorp to Vereeniging. Tony knew his products. He was polite. He took time to listen to the complaints and problems of these far-flung shopkeepers. He became Mr Traumann's top salesman. He was earning a great deal of money but still it wasn't enough.

His social life ate up the money as fast as he could earn it. Young ladies were expensive but they were worth every penny. He was out dancing most nights but Saturdays were the highlight of the week. It was the time of stovepipe suits, winkle pickers, quaffed hair and house parties. The polished cars pulled into the lot at the end of Sivewright Avenue. The girls gathered together, giggling, primping, and swapping lipsticks and gossip. The boys leaned against the cars, smoking, looking cool and discussing which party to go to. Tony always knew the best places, the parties in Linksfield and Highlands North and the not-to-be-missed events in Houghton. These were invitation-only but that didn't deter them. A party was far more fun if gatecrashed. It was also more likely to provide a fight.

Tony drove the Citroën to St Patrick's Road. His friends hung out the windows, whistling, whooping and shouting at the big houses.

"I'm going to have one of these one day."

"Look at the size of that thing. It's a bloody mansion."

"There're all the cars. The party's over there."

Tony parked the car on the curb. They piled out and started up the driveway, jostling and crowding each other. The night air echoed with a faint beat of music. The trees cast dark shadows across the moonlit lawn. Tony smelled mown grass and Brylcreem. The curved driveway brought the house into view. He stopped, gazed at its classic lines, and pillared entrance. Mercedes, Jaguars, Rolls Royces lined the turning circle. Its central pond of interlocking sandstone and ornate fountain silhouetted against the bright windows of the house. Water lilies cloaked the surface, splashed gently by the fountain. Tony felt anticipation rise in him like the bubbles in champagne. He moved towards the stone steps, bounded up them two at a time and caught up with his friends as they entered the front door.

The stone-flagged entrance hall was filled with brightly attired guests. White-linened tables bore a vast buffet. Tony grabbed a handful of pastries on his way through. They were following the sound of music, through the formal sitting room where old people shared gossip and sandwiches, down a passageway, off-leading doors firmly closed. The beat came louder. The passage widened to reveal double doors, closed but unlocked. Tony saw movement through the cottage panes, pulled open the doors and stepped onto a large paved area. The music pulsed in his ears. The crowd dancing on the terrace flowed over onto the manicured lawn that stretched to a low stone wall. A swimming pool reflected strings of coloured lights.

"Wow, look at this crowd."

"We'll blend in. They're so many people."

"I'm getting a drink.

They walked over to the marquee pitched on the lawn. Three barmen manned the long trestle tables set up to serve drinks. There were bowls of chips and popcorn. Tony sipped his Coke, took a handful of chips. The dancers spun and dipped. A blonde ponytail caught his eye. He watched it swish, tried to get a better view, waited to see her face. Distant memories of Janna flickered through his mind—but she was long gone—hooked up with some trainee auditor. The song ended. He saw her take the arm of the boy she'd been dancing with. They came into the marquee and the boy took her to a table, held her chair. He came toward the bar, brushed past Tony. Tony put down his glass and walked over to her.

"What's your name?"

"Joan."

"I'm Tony. I'm going to be taking you home."

"I'm with someone, Tony."

"Yes, you're with me."

Joan looked into the green eyes. She smiled.

"Hey, stop chatting up my date."

"I don't think she wants to be your date any more."

"Who d'you think you are? Beat it."

"Maybe you want to talk about this outside?"

"Let's go, mister. I'll be back in a minute, Joan."

Tony and Joan's escort left the marquee. They walked across the lawn towards the side of the house. As they rounded the corner the young man started to remove his jacket. Tony kicked him the crutch. The young man yelled, reached for his leg. Tony delivered an upper cut that caught him on the jaw. He staggered backwards, one arm still caught in the sleeve of his jacket. The rest of the jacket hung on the ground and he stood on it and fell onto his back. Tony was astride him, his fist raised. The young man looked up into hooded eyes.

"Get out of here. Now."

The fist descended, smashing his mouth.

Q: So that's how you met your first wife and moved to Rhodesia?

A: Yes and no. That wasn't the only fight I'd been in. I got into a lot of fights—I was an aggressive, angry young man. More of a gangster than a civilized person. *Tony glances up, eyes guarded.* Every Wednesday and Saturday night was fight night. I was part of the school's boxing team but, twice a week, I went looking for fights— guys who wanted to challenge me on the streets. But things were getting out of hand. A friend of mine's dad was a policeman—an investigator. He took me to one side and warned me, 'Tony you had better stop this fighting. One day you are going to hit someone and he is going to fall and hit his head on a rock and he's going to die. You will be up for manslaughter.' But it wasn't that easy—everyone wanted to challenge me; I had a reputation. Then one day I got into a fight with a judge's son—I put him in hospital.

Q: So you needed to get out the country?

A: Well, I needed a clean start. I married Joan and four days later we left for Rhodesia. That was on 10th April, 1947. Her stepfather was offered a job up there and he decided to take his family. He said he could probably get me work up there too. So we got married and moved to Salisbury.

Q: How did you end up in Bulawayo?

A: The company my father-in-law worked for had a branch in Bulawayo and they offered me a position as a salesman. I bought a house with my matric money, two cars, and some furniture. We lived the good life and the money just disappeared. I have never been able to live on my salary.

Q: What did you do?

A: I defrauded my insurance company.

Chapter Seven

// My ring's gone."

Joan stood on the edge of the small lake. The water ran from her hair, merged with the tears on her cheeks, and dripped from her chin. She gripped her left hand in her right, staring at her engagement finger as though at a horrible wound. Tony leapt from his chair, rushed over to his wife and took hold of her elbow. John and Lillian crowded round her. The other guests came over to see what was going on. Lillian put her arm around Joan.

"We'll find it, dear. It must be in the water. We'll all look."

"But it's so muddy. We'll never see it."

John looked at the lake. The water sparkled in the bright sunlight. A small breeze ruffled the surface and whispered in the reeds. He loved his lake; it was the reason he'd bought the property. When he'd seen the smallholding for the first time, it was the stream that ran through the middle that had attracted his attention. No one else wanted to buy the piece of land because the stream made it too difficult to plant and tend crops—but he had imagined the lake,

planned it and worked long and exhausting hours to realize his
dream of a natural swimming pool. He and Lillian had parties every
Sunday by the lake.

"Let's wait for the mud to settle a little. Then we'll divide the area
up and walk through gently. We might feel the ring with our feet."

"We'll all help, dear. I'm sure we'll find it."

The afternoon was spent trying to find the ring. The guests used
sieves and strainers, they dived and shuffled and stirred up the mud
so that the water darkened and swirled. Tony assured Joan that he
would buy her another ring and everyone said how sorry they were
but that accidents do happen.

On the way home Tony pulled into a lay-by and stopped the
car. It was almost dark, the silhouette of a farmhouse was etched
against the grey-black sky, and its lighted windows an echo of the
brightening stars. He switched off the headlights and turned to Joan
in the dark and silence of the car.

"You were brilliant."

Joan smiled, reached across the seat to put her arms around his
neck. He pulled her towards him, kissed her, tasting wine and
warmth and good living. Her hand went to his shorts, burrowed
in the warm folds of the cloth. He shifted his weight, groaned. She
withdrew her fingers, held the ring up to the fading light.

"I can never wear it again."

"When the insurance pays out I'll buy you another one."

"We need the money, don't we, Tony?"

"More than ever, now that I've lost my job."

"God, my stepfather's an idiot."

"Yes, he was stupid to hit his boss. I don't suppose he thought
they'd fire me as well, though."

"What are we going to do?"

Tony unbuttoned Joan's blouse. He bent his head to her breasts,
cupping the soft, warm flesh with his hands.

"I'll show you," he murmured as he pulled her closer to him.

❀❀❀❀❀

The insurance payout was five times the actual value of the ring. Tony's jeweller friend, who had given him the inflated valuation certificate, was happy to see them when they came in to his shop to buy a new ring. He pulled out trays of solitaires, showed Joan clusters, flawless whites nestling in diamond chips, set in white gold or platinum. Joan tried on ring after ring, holding her red-tipped fingers up to the light, admiring, adoring, wanting.

"Have you found another job yet, Tony?"

"I'm still looking for something decent. I've got a temporary position with a clothing company but I won't last long there."

"Go and see this mate of mine. He's got a cycle company. I know he's looking for a good salesman."

"Thanks, Fred. I'll call him this afternoon."

Chapter
Eight

Tony joined Rhodesia Cycles and Toys and was to stay with them for the next nine years. He received a fixed salary and a small commission. He had to use his own car although the company paid for petrol and his expenses. He became a commercial traveller just like his father.

Tony's route took him into the most rural areas where he sold his goods to trading stores, so isolated that a salesman's visit was a valued and revered occurrence. As he came to know the traders, so they invited him to stay with them, providing hospitality in exchange for stories of the cities and of other people he met on his route. Tony cultivated these friendships, not only to pocket the hotel expenses but also to meet the beautiful and lonely young women living in the rural areas. They welcomed his advances.

He started to take his camera with him and begun to build a name as a talented portrait photographer. The traders organized photographic customers for Friday afternoons and Tony would set up his equipment in a corner of the shop and photograph babies, school children and young couples and families. On his return to the area, six weeks later, he brought the mounted and framed photographs and collected the money.

He developed a unique technique in his portraits. They were modelled on the old-style sepia fade-out photographs, where there was no background, just the head and shoulders of the subject. They looked like etchings and were so popular that, when word spread, visitors from other countries became regular customers on their trips to Rhodesia.

The photography brought in good money but Tony was always on the lookout for new ways to increase his income. As he stood in the yard of one of the traders, he noticed some doors leaning up against the wall. He walked over for a closer look. They were cheap and crudely constructed, just like the doors that had been in his house when he'd first moved in. They'd been one of the first things he'd changed. He studied the way they'd been put together, took out his notebook and drew a few lines.

"How much do those doors cost you, Tommy?"

"Five pounds each."

"If I could supply them at four pounds would you buy them from me?"

"If they're as good as these, sure I would."

Tony started to make doors in the driveway of his house. He showed his gardener how to use a saw and a plane, how to smooth off the edges for a good finish. When he arrived home from his route on a Saturday morning he would kiss Joan, comment on how his daughter was growing and then call his gardener to help with the doors. They laboured all weekend to fill his orders; and then he addressed the doors with a big marker and made out the rail notes. On Monday, Joan phoned the railways to collect and deliver the orders. Tony supplied doors to ten traders in Matabeleland and supply stores in Wankie, Gwelo and Chipinga. He serviced his route for Rhodesia Cycles and Toys and collected money for doors and photographs. He was away from Monday to Saturday five weeks out of six. The sixth week he serviced the shops in and around Bulawayo and could sleep in his own bed at night. His business grew and grew, until he was earning almost nine hundred pounds a month, a top salary in Rhodesia of the sixties.

Joan wasn't happy. She was stuck at home, now with two children. She never saw her husband. When he was at home he was either in the darkroom or in the driveway. She enjoyed the money he made, bought whatever she wanted, spoilt the children but she was lonely and felt neglected. Her depression increased until sometimes she didn't even get out of bed in the morning.

"Don't wake your mummy; she's sick today," the children's maid whispered to them as she dressed them, gave them breakfast, then walked the older one to school, the little one tied to her back in a towel.

Joan dragged herself out of bed. She had to do something about feeling so bad. She would phone the doctor that her friend Melanie had told her about. She lay in the bath, washed her hair, tried to lift her spirits by breathing in the fragrance of the bath salts. Tony said she had to pull herself together. She wondered how you pulled yourself together. She sucked in her breath, tightened her chest. Was she pulled together now? The tears rolled down her cheeks and she blotted them with her wet hands.

The doctor was seeing her at midday; she had to get ready. She rinsed her hair, let out the bath water and lay in the empty bath until her body chilled in the dying temperature. Then she stood, wrapped herself in a towel and looked at the clothes in her cupboard. She couldn't decide what to wear. She'd do her make-up then and think about it. But the make-up needed to match the clothes. She picked up the hair dryer and started to dry and style her hair. That made her feel a little better. She picked out a midnight-blue shirtwaist dress, matching shoes. The make-up smoothed her complexion, brought out the violet of her eyes. Tony used to say she was a mirror for Liz Taylor. She applied lipstick, tried to smile at her reflection. She glanced at her watch, gathered her bag and went out the door.

The traffic flowed smoothly through the main street and she turned behind the city hall and found parking a few doors from the doctor's rooms. She was ushered straight in to him; he came round his desk to greet and settle her in the comfortable chair across from him.

"Why have you come to see me?"

Joan hesitated, not sure what to tell him, but his direct gaze gave her confidence and she started to talk about her inability to get up in the mornings, her tears for no reason, her short temper with her children.

"It's all right, Mrs Meyer. A lot of women feel like that. I'll give you some tablets that will help you."

The doctor wrote out a prescription and handed it to her. Joan was relieved that it hadn't been serious, thanked him and left for the pharmacy to execute the prescription.

The pills calmed her, helped her through the long, lonely days. She was glad that she'd pulled herself together and didn't see any need to tell Tony how she'd done it.

Chapter Nine

On one of his first trips 'down south' for Rhodesia Cycles and Toys, Mr Jacobson asked Tony to stop in at a particular business to collect a cheque that was now long overdue. He arrived in the little town of Essex Vale. Stores all in a line—a grocery, butchery, the cycle shop and a clothing shop. His boss had told him that some Greeks, by the name of Galinos, owned the shops and that the mother ran the butchery and her three sons ran the other shops. He decided to try first for the cheque in the cycle shop. He entered the store and stood facing a large range of toys and bicycles. At the far end of the shop was a counter and behind the counter stood a tall, well-built white man and two black men in overalls. Tony walked up to the counter.

"Good morning, Mr Galinos. My name is Tony Meyer. I'm with Rhodesia Cycles and Toys and Mr Jacobson asked me to come in and collect a cheque from you. The amount is two hundred and sixty-four pounds."

The big man came round the end of the counter. He raised his arm, pointed his finger at Tony. "Get the fuck out of my shop."

Tony took a step backwards. Then he turned to leave. He wasn't going to get involved in anything that might jeopardize his new job. He walked towards the door.

The blow to the back of his head sent him sprawling to the ground. His briefcase went flying into a stack of galvanized tin buckets. They crashed to the floor, clattering and clanging on the linoleum.

Tony pulled himself to his feet to see the man in front of him, raising his fist to slam into his mouth. Tony raised his knee and drove it into the man's crutch, following up with three blows to his jaw. The man sank to his knees and Tony double-fisted him on the top of his head. The man collapsed on the floor and lay still.

The door crashed back on its hinges and another man ran in. He glanced at the figure on the floor then jumped at Tony, his right hand clenched and ready to hit him. This man was smaller and much lighter than Tony. Tony grabbed hold of his wrist, held it tightly. The man raised his left hand, which Tony grabbed and held onto as well. The man now tried to kick him and Tony found himself pulling the man round in a circle. Before he realized what was happening the man's feet had left the floor and Tony was twirling him around by his wrists. He let him go and the man flew over the counter and crashed into the goods on the shelves behind. Small items showered down onto him as he lay on the ground.

Tony went to pick up his briefcase. He was intent on leaving. There was no way he'd ever come back to this madhouse. As he bent to pick up his case the door behind the counter opened and a large woman stepped into the shop. Her black hair was tied up in a cloth knotted on top of her head. She wore a filthy apron and held a huge meat cleaver in her hand, brandishing it above her head. The two black assistants jumped at her, grabbed hold of an arm each and held her tightly. She struggled to free herself then stopped fighting as she noticed the prone figure at her feet. She looked round at the devastation in the shop, then pushed the man on the floor before her with her toe.

"What are you doing, George?"

George hauled himself up, hanging on to the counter. He pointed to the door.

"Basil's here, mama."

Tony turned to see another man entering the shop. The man was about his size and very well built. He stood in the doorway, surveyed the goods strewn across the floor, the broken shelving, George holding himself up on the counter, then he went to the big man still lying on the floor. He bent over him, patted his face.

"Nicholas, get up."

Nicholas shook his head, climbed to his knees. He groaned, let his head hang between his arms. Basil looked at George, said something to him in Greek.

George walked to the door. The entrance was filled with people, mesmerized by the scene in the shop. He pushed the door closed then turned to help Nicholas to his feet. Basil said something else in Greek, bent to pick up a bucket.

Tony stood still. He looked at Mrs Galinos, still in the grip of the assistants. Her hand remained clenched round the cleaver.

Tony wondered how he was going to get out of there. He watched Basil picking up goods off the floor then turned towards George and Nicholas. As he turned his back he felt Basil behind him. The man jumped onto him, holding down his arms in a bear hug, circling his thighs with his legs. He was yelling at the other man in Greek and George shoved Nicholas towards Tony. It was like facing a large, angry, confused animal and Tony knew he was about to be beaten to a pulp.

He thought of the judo he'd learned as a child, all the holds that his brother had used on him, taunting him to break out. He jumped into the air, lifted his feet and came down backwards with Basil underneath him. He heard the air exploding out of Basil's lungs and felt himself being released. Basil was badly winded and no longer a danger.

Tony got to his feet. Nicholas stood in front of him, his fists raised. Tony hit him and hit him again and the man crashed to the ground and lay still. George looked at his two prone brothers, and Tony could see that he would have no more trouble with him. Mrs Galinos still stood between the two assistants.

The door swung open and two uniformed police entered the shop. The looked around at the devastation.

"Morning, George. What's going on in here?"

"Thank God you're here, Sergeant Rogers. This man just went mad and attacked us all."

The policeman walked towards Tony.

"You'll have to come down to the station with us, sir."

Tony would have gone to the ends of the earth with the policemen. He picked up his briefcase and followed them to their vehicle. They drove him to the charge office and took his statement.

He was released on his own cognizance.

Three weeks later Tony received a summons to appear in court to defend himself against a charge of assault. He engaged a lawyer in Bulawayo and they drove down to Essex Vale on the appointed day.

The courthouse was full of spectators. The Galinos family was well known and people had turned up to show their support, to satisfy their curiosity about the man who had thrashed Nicholas. When Nicholas entered the courtroom the buzz of conversation died down and there was silence as the spectators absorbed the mess his face was in. His bottom lip had been torn like a piece of paper, his nose had been broken and was dressed with plaster, and he had a long cut above his left eyebrow that had been stitched. His face was still swollen and the bruises ranged in colour from dark blue to yellow, with a few deep-red scabby welts.

When the magistrate entered he called the court to order and went through the legal preliminaries. Then the first witness was called to the stand. This was one of the black assistants and he was given the Bible and asked to swear to tell the truth. He went ahead and told the truth, answering each of the lawyer's questions and describing the course of events exactly as they had happened. The second assistant was then called to the stand and he corroborated the previous witness's statements. The attack on Mr Meyer had been unprovoked. Mr Meyer had entered the shop humbly and spoken to Mr Nicholas with respect. Mr Nicholas had gone crazy for no reason. Then Mr George came in and also went crazy. And Mr Basil had jumped on Mr Meyer's back. Mama Galinos came in with a meat cleaver. Mr Meyer was lucky he knew how to look after himself—otherwise he would be dead.

There was a buzz of conversation through the courtroom and the magistrate had to bang his gavel for silence. He glared at the spectators then glared at the Galinos family sitting with their lawyer. He then dismissed the case.

Tony drove back to Bulawayo with his lawyer.

"I'm relieved it's over, Bob. I've been put under a lot of pressure by my employer. The Greek community makes up a big percentage of TRC's customers. At least now I've been vindicated."

"Yes. You could see that the witnesses were telling the truth."

"I hear Nicholas has a bit of a reputation anyway."

"He's not the full load, Tony."

"The case has cost me money, Bob. Is there anything we can do?"

"We can sue them for malicious prosecution."

"If we win, what can we get?"

"We'll claim the damages and we could get all the costs as well."

"If you think we have a good enough chance, then I think we should take it."

"Okay, Tony. I'll get the paperwork started this afternoon."

Tony's case against the Galinos family for malicious prosecution was heard before a Bulawayo high court judge two months later. Tony won the case and was awarded damages of £2,500 and costs for both cases and Mr Jacobson finally received his cheque for two hundred and sixty-four pounds. This, together with the payout from the ring, allowed him and Joan to build their dream house.

Chapter
Ten

It was 1966.

Tony enjoyed the money he was earning. He wanted to maintain his income but started thinking about changing his job to allow him more time at home. He didn't know Joan any longer; she seemed distant, reserved and she was gaining weight. He put it down to the birth of their third child.

A friend told him about a trouser factory that was in a bit of trouble.

"The father died and left it to his wife. Their son's trying to run it but he's not doing too well."

Tony knew about trousers from his years with Traumann Trading. The clothing industry appealed to him, so he called the factory and made an appointment to see Roland Jacobson. Roland was a big man. He filled his office chair, spilled over the edges of his shirt. He had a foghorn of a voice and a hand that enveloped Tony's—damp, but solid. He knew how to make a good pair of trousers but he couldn't sell water to a dying man in the desert.

"My accountant says the firm's in trouble. We had a big market in Northern Rhodesia, but then they called themselves Zambia and closed the borders because of sanctions. That was in '64 and the business has struggled ever since."

"What about the local market, Mr Jacobson?"

"Can't break in here; too much competition. I've got my range with a firm in South Africa but they're not bringing me any orders."

"I can get this business back on its feet again."

"Lawrence said I should see you, Mr Meyer. That if anyone could turn this factory around it would be you."

"I'm due for a change. What can you offer me?"

"I'll pay you five hundred pounds, all expenses and commission on sales."

"I'm earning more than that now. I want to be your sales director. As sales director I want £2,500 per month, all expenses and an overriding commission of two-and-a-half per cent of turnover. Those are my terms."

"They're tough terms, Mr Meyer, but I'm prepared to give it a go for three months. At the end of the trial period, if I'm still losing money you leave without notice. If we mutually agree that you stay on, there'll be a three-month notice period for each of us. I'll get my lawyers to draw up a contract."

Tony worked out his notice with Rhodesia Cycles and Toys, telling his door customers that he was going on long leave. He wouldn't close that door until he was sure that the next was wide open.

His first ask for Roland Jacobson was a stock-take. He found that the factory had forty-eight thousand pairs of trousers, all broken ranges. That meant that there were sizes and colours missing from each range, so Tony decided to clear the backlog and then concentrate on what the market wanted. He railed the trouser samples to

Chapter 10

Johannesburg and followed on behind in his own car. He went to
the firm of agents that Roland was using and called a meeting of
the salesmen. He discovered that, because they knew nothing about
trousers, they concentrated on selling their vests, underpants,
T-shirts and blankets. He gave them a crash course in marketing
men's clothing and went out on the road with each one individually.
Within six weeks he had cleared the broken ranges and Roland
had to double production to keep him supplied with the stock his
salesmen were shifting daily.

He went back to Rhodesia and started working on creating a
market in Malawi.

"What about South Africa, Tony? I don't want those guys to get
slack if you're not there."

"Marketing is like a wheel that you push, Rollie. It travels on its
own momentum for a while, and then starts wobbling and falls over.
I'll be back down there just when they start wobbling, give them
another push and off they'll go again."

At the end of 1967 Tony, was called into the office for a meeting.
Mrs Jacobson, as large as her son, sat in a chair by the desk. Her
floral-print dress stretched across her massive bosom and ballooned
around her large torso like a rose garden after a hailstorm. She
clutched her white canvas bag in her lap as though afraid it might be
snatched from her grasp. Tony looked at Roland who kept his eyes
on the floor. The accountant was the only one who stood and shook
Tony by the hand.

"Please, sit down Mr Meyer."

"What's going on, Rollie?"

"We have a bit of a problem, Mr Meyer. I've called this meeting on
behalf of the Jacobsons."

"What's the problem?"

"You're earning more money than Roland, Mr Meyer."

"So what?"

"He's drawing £5,000 a month and you're getting £15,000. He owns the factory."

"Well, the way to sort it out is for Roland to draw more money."

"We want you to take a drop Mr Meyer."

"I'm not prepared to do that, Mr White."

"I'll talk to the Jacobsons and we'll let you know the outcome."

It took two months for the Jacobsons to decide that they wanted him to leave as soon as possible—they had agents set up to market their products and Tony was costing them a fortune. Tony pointed out that, according to their contract, they had to give him three months' notice but he agreed to leave his job as long as they paid his salary and the full commission on sales for the three-month period.

"No hard feelings, Rollie. It's just the way it is."

"Okay Tony. We don't have much choice. Our lawyers say we have to pay you anyway."

Tony welcomed the three months' respite. He knew just what he wanted to do. He would start his own business.

Chapter
Eleven

One sunny afternoon in April 1968, Tony bought out a small factory with some ancient machinery and Meyerton Industries was born. Tony and his friends, Jack, foreman of Westway Furniture and radio cabinet-maker, and Aubrey, invested £3,000 each, toasted each other with glasses of Asti Spumante and dreamed of how much money they were going to make.

It was not a good time to be starting a new business in Rhodesia. The economy was stagnant, stocks of various items were running out and the building trade was in a slump. Meyerton Industries was not deterred by the situation and began production of cabinets for radios, gramophones and sewing machines. It was a small beginning but Tony was full of big ideas. He wanted to make things out of wood, things that were good to look at. They also had to be practical, and expensive, to produce. He walked round his house looking at the items he lived with every day. What he hated most in his house was the kitchen. It was cheap and badly built, just like the doors that he'd replaced. He started to make drawings of a new kitchen, seeing how it could be more practical, changing the height of the counters, and sketching a cupboard that would take the length of a broom, one that was ventilated for storing vegetables. He took his drawings to the factory and they worked on the prototype. They made cabinets, costing meticulously, wasting nothing and installed the new kitchen to the delight of Joan and the envy of her friends. They started to get some orders from this first design, and the business grew very slowly, mainly through word of mouth and recommendation.

At about this time the builders in Bulawayo decided to put together a series of show houses in an effort to revive the building trade. They started by building ten houses of various designs. Tony heard about this venture and went to see the builders individually. He showed them samples of the cabinets that his factory was now producing. The builders were impressed with the quality and workmanship and Tony secured orders for eight of the ten houses, with each kitchen different. People liked the show houses and the building trade began a slow recovery. As new houses were built, Meyerton Industries was given the orders for the kitchens.

It wasn't long before the partners realized that the factory was too small and the machinery too old to cope with the work. They could use their capital investment of £9,000 to expand but, they all agreed, that it was time to build themselves a new factory. Tony approached one of the builders for whom he'd built a show-house kitchen.

"We want you to build us a factory, Dennis."

"What did you have in mind?"

"I've drawn up some plans. I'll show you."

Tony unrolled the sheets pf paper, spreading them on the desk, holding down the corners so that Dennis could see. It was all there— front elevation, side and back views, floor plans showing offices, layout of the factory floor, the ablution block with drains drawn. Electricity points were indicated. The factory took up a small part of the stand. It was placed so that extensions would be easy when the time came.

Chapter 11

"This is nice, Tony, but I don't know if the municipality will pass these plans. They're not drawn up by an architect."

"There isn't any money for an architect. In fact we haven't got much capital anyway, so we have to do a deal with you, if you want the job. We'll buy the raw materials and pay your wages and then give you ten per cent overall."

Dennis sighed. He looked at the plans for a long moment.

"We can't really turn you down, Tony. It'll allow us to keep going, keep our workers employed."

"Do we have a deal?"

"We have a deal, Tony."

Tony took the plans to the municipality. He agreed to every change they wanted, asked for their opinions continually, and engaged them fully in the design of his new factory. On the morning the plans were passed he went straight to Dennis's office.

"What's it going to cost, Dennis?"

"Give me a moment, I'll work out a price."

Dennis scratched figures on a piece of paper. He added columns, changed numbers, tapped away on his adding machine and finally sat back and looked at Tony.

"I think we can build this factory for between five and six thousand."

"I want a quote for fifteen, Dennis."

"Good God, I thought you'd try and knock me down, not treble my figure."

"Just write out the quote, Dennis. It doesn't change our deal in any way."

"No, it doesn't. Just tell me when you want us to start."

Tony's next step was the building society. He sat with the senior manager and filled out the forms to apply for a mortgage bond. He gave the manager the builder's quote and asked for the application to be dealt with urgently.

"If you would like to wait, I will ask my secretary to bring you coffee."

"That will be fine, Mr White."

The secretary led Tony to an easy chair in the front office and went into the small kitchen to make coffee. Tony picked up the *Time* magazine from the table beside him. He could see into the kitchen and he watched the secretary, busy at the counter. The high heels tightened her legs, shaped her calves, swelled her buttocks against the pencil skirt as she moved to the kettle and then over to the cupboard again. She reached up to a shelf for cups, showing off her trim waist, then bent to find a tray in the cupboard under the counter. She arranged cup, milk jug and sugar basin on the tray and reached for the kettle as it began to hiss. She filled the cup, then found a plate and shook biscuits onto it. She picked up the tray, turned toward Tony and found him watching her. A faint smile creased her cheeks as she walked towards him. Her stockings swished, the cup rattled in its saucer. She bent to place the tray on the table. Tony followed the line of her neck, a V of smooth chest descending into ample cleavage. He placed his hand on her arm and looked up into brown eyes.

"Meet me after work. I'll be at the Gatehouse."

Her smile widened, showing even white teeth. She lent towards him. He picked up the scent of jasmine.

"I'll be there at six, Mr Meyer."

Chapter
Twelve

On 11th November 1965, Ian Smith and his Rhodesian Front party unilaterally declared the country to be independent of Great Britain, from then on known as UDI, and a blatant act of white rebellion in colonial Africa. The document was a reaction to the belief that Britain was going 'to sell-out' Rhodesia's whites and that the country would follow the paths of Kenya and the Congo, whence the white refugees flooded south with stories of horror and outrage. The reaction to UDI was a total world boycott. Being a landlocked country, Rhodesia would have been dead in the water within three months. They relied on imports of oil, communications, international finance and banking and they were shut off from it all. To survive, the government did a deal with South Africa involving the use of railways and airways for trade, and the banks to move money in and out of the country. The government tried to market Rhodesia's products with little success and, in 1968, they called on their entrepreneurial businessmen to go overseas for them. These men negotiated with anyone who would buy Rhodesia's main products—

chrome, iron ore, tobacco, sugar, beef and many secondary industrial products. The government allowed them a small commission of two-and-a-half per cent, which translated into large amounts of money. They handled the banking through Switzerland and South Africa whence money was then fed back to Rhodesia.

The government realized that many citizens had access to money outside the country and they set up a system whereby certain individuals would be allowed to use this currency to buy and import items that were no longer obtainable. They could sell the goods in Rhodesia at whatever profit margin they chose. The permits became known as NCI (no currency involved) permits and anyone who was issued with them was guaranteed to make a fortune.

Tony was in Johannesburg when Joan's mother died. He called her, expecting trauma, ready to book her flight and meet her at the airport.

"Just help my stepfather arrange the funeral, Tony. I'm not coming down."

"You'll be expected, Joan."

"Make apologies. Tell them I'm not well."

The funeral was a low-key affair, attended by few family, even fewer friends. The rabbi hadn't known the deceased and kept the service short and general. As the coffin was laid in the grave, flowers were scattered on the lid and then bruised by the first shovelful of earth. The mourners repaired to Mom's house for tea and the reading of the will. Joan inherited forty thousand rand.

Tony's factory made the best kitchens in Rhodesia. The business had expanded into the export market and Tony had an agent in

South Africa who was marketing his products there. Tony went often to Johannesburg on business; saw the range of items that Rhodesians would buy in a moment. He knew exactly what he wanted to bring into Rhodesia with the windfall of Joan's inheritance—glass mosaic and white cement for the swimming pool industry.

On his return to Rhodesia he went to see the Minister of Commerce and Industry, Jack Mussett.

"Mr Mussett, I have access to forty thousand rand. I would like NCI permits."

"Very well, Mr Meyer. We will grant you the permits to bring in machinery for your factory."

"I have all the machinery I need. I want to bring in whatever I like that can be sold here."

"We can only grant you permits for machinery."

"I'm exporting a lot of goods, Mr Mussett, and bringing in much-needed foreign currency. If you won't give me the NCI permits to bring in whatever I like with my own forty thousand rand then go and fuck yourself."

Jack Mussett looked at the man sitting across from him. He saw determination and persistence. He saw a man who was not intimidated by power or authority. Rhodesia was built on people like this—pioneers and rebels. The country needed imports of every description paid for with foreign money. He was unused to being treated in this manner but he would put his country first.

"All right, Mr Meyer. The permits will be granted."

Tony submitted the application forms for Reserve Bank approval that same afternoon. He waited for his own bank to be informed that a forty-thousand-rand allocation of NCI permits was available to him. When they telephoned to say the paperwork was in order he requested a two-thousand-rand permit.

The bank kept a ledger of the amount of money granted and marked each request off the ledger. Tony received a document stating the amount. The import permit was issued against this bank form.

Tony studied his first NCI permit. It was an ordinary photostat form, stating the he could bring in two-thousand-rands-worth of goods, in rather sloppy handwriting using a common ballpoint pen. Tony looked at the pens on his desk. He picked up the nearest ballpoint, drew a line on the back of an envelope. The colour matched the pen that had been used to fill in his permit. He pulled the permit in front of him and added a naught to the R2,000. He now had an import permit to allow him to bring in two-thousand-rands-worth of glass mosaic.

In 1970, Rhodesia became a republic. The country's success in overcoming sanctions generated confidence in the future. The economy was entering a minor boom, created by the belief that the new constitution would provide long-term stability. Dissatisfied foreigners now viewed Rhodesia in a positive light as a new home, and immigrants outnumbered those emigrating. It was learnt through the grapevine that a more favourable rate of exchange could be found at Meyerton Industries than at the bank and foreign currency flowed into the safe at the factory. Tony set up a bank account in South Africa especially for direct deposits of rands; local currency in cash or bank cheques were waiting for depositors when they arrived in Rhodesia. It was a referral system that grew and grew.

Every trip that Tony made to Johannesburg saw him taking out large amounts of foreign bank notes to pay for his purchases in South Africa. He carried them in his pockets, in his briefcase and hand luggage and was never searched at the airport. Joan's forty thousand rand stayed safely invested in South Africa. He had needed it for the issuing of the permits but he certainly didn't need it to pay for the goods he took back to Rhodesia. It was his wife's money anyway. Over three years he increased his NCI permits from the original forty thousand to a massive four hundred thousand rands.

Q: But wasn't this all highly illegal?

A: Of course, but who was it hurting? No one, that's who. The country was benefiting and I was getting rich. What's wrong with that?

Chapter
Thirteen

It was 1971.

The kitchen market grew, money became available for expansion and Tony decided it was time to branch out into the furniture industry. Meyerton Industries bought some specialized machinery and began to produce lounge suites. They employed an upholsterer and a manager/salesmen to run that section of the company.

Don Evans was full of enthusiasm and energy and couldn't wait to get started in his new job. He had experience in the retail furniture trade and loved the design side of the industry. His new job was full of opportunity and he wanted to make the most of it. As soon as they had some samples Tony set up his photography equipment and they put together a small catalogue. Then, armed with his list of retailers, Don Evans went out on the road to bring in his first orders.

It was a very different man who returned after three days. He hadn't booked a single order.

"Why won't they buy from us, Don?"

"They want ninety days' credit, Tony. The buyer from OK Bazaars wants a kickback and he wasn't the only one. They're all sharks."

"We don't have the cash flow for ninety days. And I'll tell you now, Don, I will never do business with anyone who wants a kickback."

"I went to every retailer. It was the same story with all of them."

"We'll find a way round them. In fact, bugger them all, we'll sell direct to the public."

"That's a bloody good idea, Tony. But how can we do that?"

"Leave it to me, Don. Just get on with making some beautiful lounge suites."

Tony called in a local artist. His brief was straightforward.

"I want a sketch of each piece of furniture. Put it in a homely setting, just as if it were in someone's lounge."

While he waited for the artist's drawings he rearranged the factory. They had built big in the first place and had room to section off part of the space. Tony had a builder put in a door to the new area and it now had its own entrance. Then they brought in the furniture samples and laid them out in separate displays. Tony set up a desk and seating area for Don where he could take orders. Meyerton Industries had its first showroom.

When the artwork was done he took it to the newspaper and took out an advertisement. 'DIRECT TO THE PUBLIC' was the banner over the artist's drawing. Every week the advertisement would show a different illustration.

Tony could keep his prices really low. He had no middleman, no retailers to carry for thirty days. He set his prices at two-and-a-half per cent above wholesale.

Factory shops were unheard of in 1971 and the public flocked to Meyerton Industries, intent on seeing what this new form of shopping was all about. There was an outcry from the retailers and within a short space of time Tony had a visit from the municipality.

"You are not allowed to trade in the industrial areas, Mr Meyer. You have to have a licence."

"Can I have a showroom here?"

"Yes, but you cannot do business from your showroom."

Tony called his friend Daniel Mailer. Dan owned an electrical business. Tony had put some money into Dan's company when he'd helped set it up a year before. He was a silent partner but they often got together to discuss business matters over lunch or an evening drink. They agreed to meet for lunch at Victoria Hotel.

The restaurant was on the top floor and Tony and Dan were shown to a table at the window.

"I hear your factory showroom is cleaning up, Tony?"

"It's doing well but the municipality's on my back."

"What's their problem?"

"They say I have to have a licence to trade in the industrial sites and they refuse to grant me one."

"Bloody typical of the bureaucratic mindset."

"Yeah, well I've got an idea that'll stuff them. That's why I asked you to lunch. It involves the electrical business."

"You know I'll do anything to help, Tony."

Tony looked down at the cars making their way along Selbourne Avenue. The road bisected the park and he loved to drive that route through the landscaped gardens. He could see the layout from his vantage point—the pathways like pale snakes moving through a green swath, joining at the fountain, meeting at the monument. The palms were foreshortened from this height but still striking. He turned back to Daniel.

"I think we should open an electrical shop in town."

"But I'm not a retailer."

"It's not going to be a retail outlet. You stick one of your guys in to sell a few plugs and things. I'll put some furniture in there to make it look nice. It'll really be an office for one of my salesmen. He'll have furniture catalogues and prices but he'll be sending the buyers to the factory showroom."

"Brilliant idea. So all the adverts will give the town address, then the municipality can't touch you."

"That's what I had in mind."

"Let's go see what's available to rent. I'm a hundred per cent behind you, Tony."

Dan had the shop up and running within a few weeks. He stocked it, initially, with electrical items but soon found that it was worthwhile to carry small appliances like kettles, toasters and hairdryers. He sold them to the furniture buyers who returned to the electrical shop with their order sheets. They came to put down their deposits and arrange for delivery—and generally walked out with items from the shop.

Meyerton Industries delivered within a week of order in the first few months of business. As the public caught on to this new way of buying and the big savings they made, by cutting out the middleman, so the orders increased. The factory had to concentrate more and more on furniture and started to expand their range. When delivery delay ran to four weeks Tony knew it was time for expansion once again. He increased his per centage to five and then ten per cent above wholesale to pay for the increased work force. The orders continued—their name for exceptional quality and value for money spread and Meyerton Industries opened a huge showroom in Salisbury.

Q: And then?

A: I started to go overseas on business more and more. I was one of about a dozen businessmen who negotiated deals for Rhodesian goods with Eastern Europe, Japan, England, America … anyone who'd buy our products.

Q: Even in the face of sanctions it was business as usual?

A: Rhodesia was a reliable trading partner and could offer enough incentive for foreign countries to disregard UN embargoes. We were doing our duty by winning the economic war for our country—but we were also making a lot of money.

Q: You earned two-and-a-half per cent on these deals?

A: Yes, it translated into plenty of dollars. Only Rhodesia's capacity to supply or buy limited this income. I loved travelling and I was learning about international finance and Swiss banking and I was making useful contacts.

Q: How was the factory doing?

A: It was growing at a great rate. We put more and more money back in and kept expanding. We had to keep showing a loss to the taxman. I had a brilliant accountant, Ronnie Ruttenberg.

Q: So, everything was going well for you?

A: *Tony sips his orange juice, breaks a muffin into small pieces.* Aubrey died at about that time.

Q: He was your third partner?

A: Yes, bit of a schlepper but a good man. It was unexpected; he had a heart attack. We paid out his wife and then it was just me and Jack.

Q: How did that affect your business?

A: It's easier when there're just two people making decisions. It's also safer. We were involved in a lot of deals.

Q: Currency deals?

A: That's how I made my big money.

Q: How did it work?

A: We would pay a third of the value. That was the rate from the beginning. Let's say they had a hundred thousand Rhodesian dollars. We would pay them thirty-three thousand Rhodesian dollars worth of foreign currency. They could have it deposited in any country. There was a huge risk; it was highly illegal.

Q: You all took the risk anyway?

A: I took the risk. All the others would have denied everything if I'd been caught.

Q: And were you caught?

Chapter
Fourteen

The year was 1973.

Tony poured himself a Coke, added two ice cubes and a slice of lemon. He stood at the window and looked at the city. The sun was setting and the streets were cloaked in gold and evening shadow. He sipped slowly, feeling the minutes tick by. He watched the cars filling the narrow streets ten storeys below. The traffic was hardly moving. A haze of hot exhaust shimmered above the cars, leaving a black residue on the buildings, spores in the lungs of hurrying pedestrians.

He checked his watch again; it was almost five thirty. They weren't coming; he was sure of it now. He would have to call Jack.

He sat on the edge of the chair, dialled the number quickly. Jack's wife answered after many rings. Her voice was pinched and low.

"Tricia, it's Tony. I need to speak to Jack."

"They're here, Tony."

"Who's there, Tricia? What's happening?"

"It's the CID, Special Branch. They're going through everything."

"I have to talk to Jack. Get him for me."

The Coke tasted stale. He put the glass on the table.

"He can't come to the phone, Tony. He says to tell you it's all over, that they know everything and you'd better come home."

Tony rested the phone in its cradle and reached for the phone book. He found the number, waited for the phone to be answered.

"When's the next flight to Johannesburg?"

"Ten tonight, sir, but it's pretty full. I'll see if there are seats available."

Tony leaned back in the chair, looked at the heavy linen curtains. They were thick and full and framed the big window. The cream fabric glowed in the gold of the sunset. A heavy shadow from the building next-door spilled over the windowsill to envelop his feet.

"I have two seats left, sir."

"They're mine, then. My name is Tony Meyer; my companion is Sandra Campbell."

"Right, sir. Check-in time is two hours prior to departure. Enjoy your flight."

Tony had always loved Zurich. Now his ten days here had just been reduced to an afternoon. He pushed away from the chair, stretched his arms above his head and turned towards the bedroom. He opened the door and stepped onto the carpet. His bare feet embraced the thick pile. The expanse of white ended at the big four-poster, which was wreathed in layers of royal and azure. He stood in the doorway, regarding the woman reading on the piled-up pillows. Her long legs were as shapely as when she had made coffee for him, at the building society five years previously. Her slip etched the shape of her breast; its whiteness echoed the snowy carpet. He walked to the foot of the bed, held out his hand. Sandy smiled, turned away to put her book on the bedside table. The satin slip slid up her thigh, revealing darkness at the curve of her bottom. Tony reached for her hand, pulled her to the carpet and felt her yield in his arms. Immediately all thoughts of the business and his impending return to Rhodesia faded.

Airports had always held an excitement for Tony and he still felt a thrill, even after years of flying. The airport in Johannesburg was big and ugly, but it was familiar and comfortable too. He put Sandy on the first flight to Bulawayo. He wanted to get her home with her husband; this business trip no longer needed a secretary.

"I'll give you a cheque for a month's salary."

"You don't have to, Tony. We've only been gone a couple of days. It's not your fault what's happened."

"No, but it's the deal I did with Dave. He'll expect you to be paid, whatever. I don't want him getting possessive about his wife."

"Okay, then. When do you think you'll get back?"

"I don't know. I'll find out what's happening first."

Tony kissed her and watched her walk to the departure lounge. The soft, silk blouse and snug skirt showed off her good figure, firm legs. She stopped at the door, raised her hand in a half salute. He smiled, turned away towards the lift to the parking area. His car was easy to pick out in the long-term parking. The sleek, sporty Mercedes was an earlier acquisition when he'd realized he would be spending a lot of time in South Africa. The thrill of possessing such a beauty never left him.

He eased the car into the midday traffic. Johannesburg beckoned on the horizon and Tony overtook the slower cars. As the road cleared he put his foot down, not caring about speed traps. The grass was dry and yellow on the roadside. Across the veld the feet of pedestrians on criss-crossing footpaths raised a faint dust. The winter sun warmed the car as Tony drove through the suburbs and pulled into his mother's driveway. Mom was never surprised when he turned up on her doorstep. Like the old days when dad was still alive. She just let him in, asked what he wanted for dinner.

"I'm going to kip for an hour, Mom, then I have to make some calls. I don't know how long I'm staying."

"Whatever is fine with me. I'm going to the shops. You look like you need a nice home-cooked meal."

Tony took off his shoes and lay on the bed in the spare room. It was very different from the room he had been in yesterday. Floral fabric comforters cloaked the twin beds. The heavy wooden headboards supported a single pillow each. The window drapes, in the same floral fabric, framed dull net curtains, keeping the interior safe from prying eyes. It was Mom's project, this house. He had let her choose just what she wanted. He'd taken her to the bank and arranged a chequebook for her. She had taken months to furnish it—though it still wasn't finished.

At five Tony showered and changed. He went through to the kitchen, poured himself a drink and took it into the study. He sat at the desk and pulled the phone closer. He couldn't phone Jack direct. His line might be bugged. Tony called his neighbour over the road. He could depend on him.

"Lionel, do me a favour. Go down to Jack's house. Tell him to find a safe phone, call me back on this number."

"Sure, Tony. Bulawayo's buzzing. What've got yourself into this time?"

"You'll find out soon enough. Just get Jack for me."

Tony walked around the house while he waited for Jack to call. There were souvenirs, ornaments, and photographs on every surface. He studied the photographs, family snaps from when he was a kid, now faded and old, pictures of his children, taken by himself, mounted and given to Mom on each child's birthday. He moved to the window and looked at the garden. Even the garden had knick-knacks. He could see the fishpond, the water forever cycling through a shell in the crook of a child's elbow. A green pottery frog guarded the birdbath, plaster figures peered from the ground cover, and wind chimes glinted in the late sun.

The smell of chicken roasting reminded him that he hadn't eaten since breakfast. He breathed in the aroma, thought of Mom's chicken—brown skin salty and crisp, flesh tender and white. There would be roast potatoes, green beans and pumpkin and that thick, brown gravy that only Mom knew how to make. He glanced at the clock above the fireplace. Mom liked to eat early. He wouldn't have to wait long.

The phone rang and he turned away from the window and crossed the room to the study door. He slid into the chair behind the desk, grabbed the telephone.

"This deal was one hundred per cent, Jack. What the hell went wrong?"

"You're not going to believe this, Tony."

"Have we lost the money?"

"It looks like we're right in the shit. Those bloody foreigners go to Issie's shop and tell him they want to buy a million-dollars-worth of jewellery. Issie's excited and when he goes to his Thursday night poker game he tells his mates about this great deal he's about to do. He finds the same men have approached all the jewellers in Bulawayo with the same deal."

"Why the hell do they want to buy jewellery?"

"Well, Issie phones his uncle in Salisbury to make sure he's got stock—in case they need extra—and they find that these guys have been to the jewellers there too."

"Sounds like a bloody set-up."

"That's what they thought, so they panicked and called the CID."

"Oh, shit, so that's how Special Branch got involved."

"Yeah. Burrell's lot picked up the guys three days ago. These arseholes tell Burrell it wasn't their money, it was our money and they were going to buy the jewellery and take it out the country for us and that you're waiting for them in Switzerland."

"Jesus, what's Burrell say?"

"He says he's going to get us on currency dealing. It looks like he made a deal with them. He kept one in jail and brought the Aussie to my office yesterday. I had no idea. It looked like everything was going to plan. I opened the safe to show him the money. I was about to phone you to tell you that everything was fine this end and then the fucking cops turned up. Jeez, I got a fright."

"They were going to rob us. If the cops hadn't got involved they would have stolen the money from you. That's why the Dutchman never turned up here. They were going to fucking rob us."

"Well, the cops have got the money now. They went through my house; they've got warrants for everything. When are you coming back?"

"I'll have to think about it. Get Charles to phone me. He's our fucking lawyer. He must handle this."

Tony sat at the table with Mom, half listening to her talk about food prices. It was funny how poverty made you look at what things cost, even when you no longer had to worry. The knife and fork were cool and solid in his hands, part of the silver service he'd given her as a house-warming present. He savoured the food and thought about the deal. He had been so sure it was watertight. If the other side hadn't been crooks it would have worked so smoothly. He thought back to the day they'd come to see him. Just walked into his factory; said they'd heard through the grapevine that he was the man.

"I made a pie for you. I got cream, sweet cream; you love cream."

"Thanks, Mom. I'm glad I don't live with you any more. I'd be the size of a house."

"Huh, growing boy, you need looking after."

"I'll just get the phone. Then I'll have pie with you. Lots of cream."

Tony closed the door quietly and picked up the phone.

"It's Charles, Tony. You blokes are in big shit. I'll struggle to keep you out of jail."

Tony felt his heart pump. He sat in the chair, leant over the desk, cupping the phone in his hands.

"Then I'm not coming back."

"Don't be silly. You've got a wife and kids. You might only have to serve a few years."

Tony thought about Joan and the children. His whole life was in Rhodesia, his family, his business, his friends.

"What about the money?"

"You've lost that."

Tony's chin rested on his chest. He closed his eyes.

"Okay, Charles. I'll come back, but only if Burrell agrees not to arrest me at the airport. I'll come to the office on Monday."

"Good. I'll pick you up. We'll talk then. Let me know which flight you're on."

Tony went to bed early, slept like a log. Mom brought him coffee at eight and he showered and dressed and sat with her on the stoep for breakfast. He felt calm but very, very alert, like when he was setting up deals. His brain arranged all the things he needed to know, all the things he needed to do. It seemed to lay them out in an order he could see so clearly. Charles was clever. Jack would shut up. Between them all they'd work out something. Mom let him have his thoughts, just filled his cup then went to let the maid in.

The plane landed on time in Bulawayo. Charles was waiting on the tarmac and they went into the light aircraft hangar behind the terminal.

"I have to take you straight to Burrell. Tell me about this deal so I know which deck I'm playing with."

Tony told him about the two men coming to the factory.

"They had ten million Swiss francs to sell. They wanted Rhodesian dollars. I said I'd think about it. The deal was tight too, very simple. I go to Switzerland, the Dutchman comes to my hotel there, with the Swiss francs. Jack has the dollars in our safe here and the Aussie meets him in our office. Jack phones me at four o'clock; we've got codes worked out."

"Where'd you get the money?" Ten million bucks is a hell of a lot."

"Investors. Everyone wants money out the country."

"Yeah, but that much in cash? You can't cash cheques in the banks—they have to advise the government."

"Well, that's the good part. Two weeks it took me, just two weeks to raise the cash. I thought about who had lots of cash. It's the retailers, of course. The shops take cash every day. The investors gave me some signed, blank cheques and I bought cash from the retailers."

"Those investors are not going to be happy. Burrell's got the cash now."

"Better Burrell than the crooks."

"What cut were you going to take?"

"My usual. They'd get a third of the value."

"Well, I'm glad I organize my own foreign exchange. That's quite a cut."

"I have to find some way to pay the fees you charge."

Tony grinned at Charles. They had been friends a long time.

"Okay. Let's get going. This is how we'll handle it. They'll sit over there and we sit this side of the desk. Every time they ask you a question you look at me and say, 'Charles must I answer that?' and I'll say, 'No'. Then we'll see what happens."

They picked up Tony's luggage in the terminal and headed for Charles's car. Tony looked out the window at the flat farmlands—neat squares of vegetables under irrigation, rows and rows of sugar cane, tobacco in the distance. They entered the northern suburbs of the city, then the neat grid of the centre of Bulawayo. Charles found parking and they headed to the offices of the CID.

Detective-Inspector Burrell, ex-captain of the national rugby team, was a tough, no-nonsense policeman. He ran his department with discipline and humour, a mix that endeared him to his men. He was waiting for Tony and Charles in his office.

"Good day, gentlemen. Glad you could make it, Mr Meyer. Please have a seat."

Two chairs were lined up at the desk. They sat down. A young policeman brought in a tray of coffee. "Help yourselves, gentlemen."

Detective Gordon came in and closed the door. He greeted Tony and Charles and sat down next to Inspector Burrell. He put his clipboard on the desk. The top sheet of foolscap paper was covered in cramped writing.

He started the interrogation, reading from his pages. He drew a line though each question as Tony declined to answer. Inspector Burrell sat with his arms folded on the desk. After a while he got up and walked to the window. He stood there for a long time, facing away from the scene in the room. Then he came back to his chair, stood behind it with his hands on the worn leather.

"All right, Detective Gordon, we're not getting anywhere. I'm not wasting another four hours on this nonsense. I want all your passports, Mr Meyer. You are not to leave Bulawayo until this case is cleared. My men will accompany you home to search your house and your business premises. They have a warrant."

Charles drove Tony home. The afternoon traffic was light and in a few minutes they were in the suburbs. Large trees shaded the pavements where children rode their bicycles and nannies took babies and dogs for their afternoon walk. Charles drove slowly, turned into Tony's driveway and parked the car.

"I don't think he really has anything apart from those guys' testimony. He doesn't know where the money came from. He can't prove that it was leaving the country. But he's a very sharp cookie. Don't take him lightly, Tony."

"I never make a move without you, Charles."

He watched in the rear-view mirror as the police van pulled in behind them.

"If that were true you wouldn't be in trouble now. I'm just going to check their warrants."

Joan met Tony at the front door. She was ashen, pale, the lustrous dark hair a contrast to her wan face.

"My god, Tony, I can't stand this. They say there are millions involved. There's talk of jail. I don't know how much more of this I can take."

"You always have to worry so much. Just stay with the police while they search the house. Make sure they don't pinch anything … or plant anything. Charles and I are going to have a drink."

❁❁❁❁❁

Four months later Tony got a call from Bob Burrell.

"Mr Meyer, I'd like to see you."

"I'm in my office all afternoon; you can meet me here."

Inspector Burrell arrived with Detective Gordon. The receptionist brought them to Tony's office, then left, closing the door behind her.

"Mr Meyer, I'll get right to the point. We have spent four months investigating this case. We know that you don't have ten million dollars. We know that your businesses don't have ten million dollars. The money came from elsewhere and we want those people, the investors who're trying to get money out the country. If you turn State's evidence we'll let you off all the charges.

'"Let me think about it, Inspector Burrell."

After they had left, Tony went over to Jack's office. They discussed Burrell's offer.

"I'll organize the guys to meet at my house at six, Tony."

"Tell them to bring their wives. It'll look like a social evening. We'll sort out the business and then have a couple of drinks."

That evening Jack's driveway filled with cars. The wives sat on the verandah, watching the children play in the garden. Tony and Jack saw the investors in the study. Tony closed the door.

"Listen, gentlemen. Burrell came to see me today. He's offered us a deal. Jack and I can get off the charges if we turn State's evidence. He wants you guys and he wants us to give him your names."

"Jeez, Tony, you wouldn't do that, would you?"

"It's up to you guys. Jack and I have discussed it and we're prepared to take the rap, on condition that you support our families. That means fifteen thousand dollars for Joan and the same for Tricia each month and, on top of that, you cover our expenses."

"That sounds like a pretty fair deal, Tony. I'll go with it."

"Me too."

"And me."

"We're all in. Thanks, Tony, Jack. If they manage to put you in jail, you can be sure we'll look after your families."

Tony took the long way home, opened up the car on the quiet stretches of road. He relaxed into the soft leather of the seat, watched the road, and enjoyed the skill needed to ease the car smoothly round the bends. When he pulled into his driveway he saw that the lights were out downstairs. He parked the car, turned off the engine, listened to the quiet after the throaty roar. The engine tick, tick, ticked as it cooled.

He let himself in the front door, went through to the kitchen and found an ice-cold Coke in the fridge. He took down two glasses, filled them with ice cubes, put a slice of lemon in each, then made sure the doors were locked and the lights switched off. He looked in on the kids who were all fast asleep.

Joan was reading and he sat next to her and put the glasses down on the bedside table. She smiled, leant forward to kiss him. He put his arms round her, pressed the icy Coke bottle against her back. She shivered and he felt her body tighten, her hands went to his shoulders as if to push him away. She slid her fingers under his shirt and pulled it roughly over his head. He had to let go of her, let go of the bottle, which rolled on the mattress and rested against her bottom. The condensation left a dark mark on the sheet. Tony pushed her back, lifted her hips to get the bottle and rubbed it over her breasts. Her nipples pressed against the fabric of her nightie, now wet with the moisture from the bottle and clinging to her flesh. Tony leaned forward, rolled the bottle along her belly and followed the trail of moisture with his lips.

In the morning Tony met with Bob Burrell. He told him that he and Jack had thought about his offer and had decided against turning State's evidence.

"When this is all over, Bob, you will be six inches tall and I will be seven feet above you. Do what you have to!"

Chapter
Fifteen

In downtown Bulawayo a new building was going up on the corner of Fourteenth Avenue and Fife Street. Friar Tuck's, a steakhouse, was built on Fife Street and four shops went up from the corner along Fourteenth Avenue. Eighteen bachelor flats were built above the restaurant and shops. Tony's factory built and installed the kitchens and cupboards. Tony decided to take two of the shops. He moved the retail outlet for his furniture showroom into one and he and Dan moved the electrical business into the other. Discount Electrical had grown and needed bigger premises for the fridges and stoves they now stocked. Although locally made, supply did not keep up with demand and on Tony's next trip to South Africa he went to see his old friend, Tony Factor, about importing electrical goods into Rhodesia. They came to an agreement for one million rands-worth of electrical items and Tony paid the amount in full. Tony Factor agreed to provide Tony with a second invoice for half the amount for Customs purposes and Discount Electrical paid duty on this invoice.

Tony had done this many times before and he and Dan had always made sure that these false invoices were disposed of as well as the falsified NCI documents.

When Tony and Dan were summonsed to appear in court, they found that they were now charged with defrauding Customs. Among the paperwork that the police had taken from Dan's safe, along with the ten million dollars, was a file that contained the false invoice and altered NCI permit on the electrical deal.

Tony and Charles had a drink together the evening before the court appearance.

"Why aren't they charging us with currency dealing, Charles?"

"Maybe they're going to get you on this Customs deal first. Then they'll have a bit of bargaining power to persuade you to give up the investors."

"I'd never do that."

"I know that, Tony. But people give up their grandmothers to stay out of jail. They might think it's their lever."

"We've been careful for three years. We burnt documents after every NCI deal. I don't know why we didn't this time."

"There's nothing you can do about it now. Let's go to court and see what happens."

Tony and Dan each had their own lawyer but they stood up in the dock together and pleaded guilty to the charge. They listened as the police led with their evidence. They refused to reply to anything and refused to be cross-examined. The state attorney summed up his case and then their lawyers pleaded for them. The judge sat immobile throughout the proceedings, listening to the evidence and the legal argument. He set a date for sentencing and dismissed the court.

The Chronicle is Bulawayo's daily newspaper. Its reporters were delighted to have a story involving large amounts of money and well-known, local businessmen. It made a change to the ususal politics.

In the course of their investigations they discovered that Tony Meyer carried the lease on number 18, Fourteenth Avenue. This was one of the bachelor flats above the business premises his company rented on the ground floor.

The reporters managed to gain access to the bachelor flat and immediately summoned a photographer to record what they had found.

The flat was red. Everything was red. The walls were painted red, the curtains were red, the carpet was red. The small kitchen contained a well-stocked bar, lots of glasses and nothing else. The serving hatch had been widened to make a counter and four barstools, upholstered in red leather, were arranged along the front. The main room was taken up by a huge bed, sunk with brass railings into the floor. The bed had a plushly upholstered headboard and footboard in a soft, red fabric and was made up with red satin sheets.

The Chronicle ran a piece the next day below a banner headline that read, 'BROTHEL IN CITY CENTRE'. A rather unclear picture of the bed was used to reinforce the headline. Tony admitted to renting the flat but denied any involvement with illegal sexual activities.

"It's a love nest," he said, but declined to elaborate.

Tony and Dan's social circle named the flat 'Friar Fucks'.

Tony and Dan appeared in court for sentencing and were found guilty of falsifying documents and defrauding Customs. They were given a five-year suspended sentence and fined $500,000 each. They also had to pay a penalty of three times the Customs duty.

Two weeks later, Bob Burrell walked into Tony's office. Detective Gordon followed, carrying two suitcases.

"I'm returning your ten million dollars, Mr Meyer. Please make sure it's all there."

"Thank you, Inspector."

"We know this was a currency deal. We don't have enough evidence to convict you but we'll be watching you."

"My dealings are all above board, Inspector."

"So you'd have me believe."

Tony called Dan and they set up another social evening at Dan's house for the investors.

"Good evening, gentlemen. As you know, the police did not have enough evidence to convict us on the currency deal. They did manage to put together another case and we have had to pay fines and penalties. We could have walked away from all this, turning you in but we kept your names out of it."

"We're grateful, Tony."

"The police have returned the money. We're giving you back seventy cents in the dollar. That will completely cover our fines and expenses, plus a little extra for our trouble. Is everyone happy?"

"I'm not. I want my original amount back. I don't see why I should pay for your fine on a completely separate case."

"We understand, Selwyn. I'll tell Bob Burrell that you'll collect the full amount from him."

"What do you mean? You know I can't go to him for the money."

"You'll have to if you want the amount. We're only giving back seventy per cent."

"It's your choice, Selwyn."

"It's no choice, Tony. I'm over a barrel. I'll take the seventy cents."

"As long as you're sure, Selwyn."

"It's no choice, Tony."

"Okay. We'll bring each of you your share tomorrow."

A few weeks later Tony read in *The Chronicle* that the State had won a case against two foreigners, charged with conspiracy to commit a crime. The men were sentenced to four years in jail and had begun their sentences in Khami State Prison that morning at eight o'clock. Upon reading this news, Tony was able to breathe a huge sigh of relief, and allowed himself a wry smile.

Chapter
Sixteen

It was 1975.

Joan picked up the glass, noticed how the light shining through the amber liquid turned her fingers to gold. She leaned forward to hold the glass in the rays of sunlight slanting through the window and watched the reflections dancing round the room. She slid onto the carpet and lay in a patch of the warmth, holding the glass above her in both hands. Her diamond engagement ring sent shards of brilliance across the ceiling and she moved her hands and watched the yellows and whites dance over the furnishings.

The walls were papered in rose-patterned paper to the picture rail. Painted the palest pink above it. The ceiling was white with a glass crystal light like a small chandelier. The curtains were the same pattern as the wallpaper, matching Sanderson prints that she had brought back from Johannesburg some years before. She had found a local artist who painted detailed florals and had bought his watercolours for the walls, framing them in pale green and cream. The chair and bedspreads were in plain pink fabric with floral-print

cushions. The room faced north and was always sunny. It was the
spare room, twin beds for visitors, a bathroom across the hall. It was
Joan's favourite room and she used it as her haven.

She also used it to stash her pills, small white daytime pills and
green and white capsules for nighttime. The doctor also prescribed
those tiny white pills that looked like artificial sweeteners and Joan
like to think they were there to help when she felt really sour. The
golden liquid was in the bedside cabinet with the pills.

Joan was not having a good day. She'd already gone over her limit
with the daytime pills and the sweetener wasn't having an effect
either. The alcohol was making her feel sick and she had to organize
dinner. It must be getting late and then the kids would be home. She
wondered what time Tony would be home.

It was a small jump to imagine him coming home much, much
later, smelling of another woman, but still wanting her. The darkness
seeped over her like molasses.

She took a gulp of the whisky, wanted to retch. Why didn't she
just stay here, in this room, snuggle into its warmth and softness like
a mouse hiding for the winter. Another image swam into her mind,
the redness swelled up behind her eyes, making her heart beat faster,
her limbs shiver. It happened when she stood in the supermarket, not
knowing what to buy for dinner, when she met a girlfriend for lunch
and looked at the menu. She tried to blot it out with the little pills,
drown it in the whisky, but it wouldn't go away. She saw the redness
of that bed, the words describing a room she'd never seen but was
etched in her brain forever. She couldn't go on much longer, she'd
fought it for two years and now she was tired of the fight.

Joan heard the front door slam and the noisy teenage voices and
pulled herself from the floor. She put the glass and bottle in the
bedside table, turned the key and put it in her pocket. She stood at
the mirror, straightened her blouse and smoothed her skirt, then
walked across the passage to the bathroom and closed the door. She
rinsed her mouth, patted her face with water and dabbed it dry on a

towel. Hoping the whisky on her breath would not betray her.

Then she went down the passage to the kitchen to organize the staff for dinner.

Tony arrived home and sat with his family for the evening meal. Joan was quiet again but the kids more than made up for it.

After dinner they watched TV; then the children went to bed and he and Joan sat in the lounge together, alone. Tony glanced through the newspaper but nothing caught his eye. He looked up at Joan, who had left her chair and was standing at the sideboard. She was watching him.

"I'm going to bed, Tony, but I've decided to move into the spare room."

"What do you mean?"

"I mean just that. I'm moving into the spare room."

Tony got up and moved towards Joan. His arms hung at his sides but his fists were as tight as the line of his jaw.

"You'd better explain yourself, Joan."

"I'll continue to run this house. I'll look after the children. I'll carry on being a good wife to you in every way but I won't sleep with you any longer."

Tony grabbed Joan by the arms. He pushed her up against the wall.

"Who the hell do you think you are—telling me what you will and will not do."

"I won't sleep with you any longer, Tony."

Tony pushed Joan along the wall. He shoved her out the door into the hallway.

"You think you can dictate to me! Get out, you bitch! You don't sleep in my bed, you don't sleep in my house."

Tony opened the front door and pushed her outside. The door slammed behind her.

Q: Then what happened?

A: I threw her out.

Q: Why?

A: She said she wouldn't have sex with me any longer.

Q: Did you reconcile?

A: No, I fucking didn't. It had been coming for two years.

Q: You knew your marriage was breaking up?

A: She never got over the brothel article in the paper. I knew about the pills by then and they'd completely changed her.

Q: Where did she live when she moved out?

A: She stayed with the neighbours. She came into the house after I left for work and was out before I got home.

Q: You knew about that?

A: I didn't care, as long as she stayed away from me. She wanted to go back to South Africa so I bought her a house, set her up financially and she moved there with the kids.

Q: You'd met your second wife by then?

A: I met Renée three weeks after I threw Joan out. We got married at the end of 1976. I got back into the currency dealing, full blast, in 1977.

Chapter
Seventeen

In September 1976, a group of professionals and businessmen sent out a publication expressing their support for a multi-racial government and their hope for the removal of discrimination. It was later modified to ask for the introduction of majority rule. All Rhodesians were asked to subscribe to it. In contrast with this positive effort for change was the fact that the bush war was escalating and attacks on white families and African peasants were becoming increasingly more vicious. By the middle of 1977, the cost of living had risen sharply, sales tax had increased from ten to fifteen per cent; a ten per cent income tax surcharge was implemented and the war now accounted for twenty-six per cent of government expenditure. White Rhodesians were emigrating at a rate of about a thousand a month. The government reduced the emigration allowance from five thousand to one thousand dollars and overseas travel allowance from four hundred to two hundred dollars per year.

Tony had continued to grow his businesses and had avoided any illegal deals in the years since his conviction. He had large export orders and travelled to Johannesburg every month to service his South African customers. Renée loved to travel and always went with him. She introduced Tony to camping and he bought a camper they used on weekend trips to local campsites.

Tony considered the situation in the country and the desperation of people to have money outside of Rhodesia and he decided that he would resume his currency operations. It was an opportunity from which he could not turn away and he determined to learn every lesson from 1973. He would leave no paper trail and he would deal with just one reliable contact from each community.

Tony targeted three communities in Rhodesia. He spoke to his good friend, Saul. They met for an early drink at Tony's house.

"Let the Jews know that currency will be available to them out of the country, Saul. You don't know who or how."

"What sort of amounts can you get out, Tony?"

"Whatever they want. Just bring me the cash and details of where they want it deposited."

"What rate will you give?"

"Three to one on the bank rate. That's the deal."

"And I get commission?"

"You're the link; you'll get the commission. But you'll take the rap if we get caught. I've set this up so nothing leads back to me."

Tony's link with the Greeks was Costa, and the Indians came to visit him via Ishmail Naidoo. Tony spoke to Jack about the way he was going to set up the deals.

"We're going to export at one third of the price, Jack. We continue to sell at the full price in South Africa but our CDI forms will only show a third. In case we're audited here, you must reduce all our cost sheets by two thirds. To confuse the issue we do all our costings in metric from now on."

"No one's used to metric but do think it's confusing enough?"

"It will be, especially as we're not going to do a true conversion."

"What do you mean, Tony?"

Chapter 17

"It'll sound right because four thousand and fifty millimetres sounds a lot and will only be eighteen inches. We'll see if they pick up on it."

"I know, Jack."

"So our export documents will show a third and that's what we'll bring back here?"

"That's it. The rest we'll leave in South Africa to provide money for Rhodesians who want funds out of the country."

"We might end up with cash flow problems, Tony."

"I've thought of that. I've worked out a six-year game plan. We don't sell the whole lot. The first year we leave twenty per cent in an account, second year—forty per cent, third year—sixty per cent. By the fifth year we shouldn't have to touch that two-thirds syphon. That'll be our contingency fund."

"Okay, Tony, you've got it all worked out. I'll go and see about the cost sheets."

"Jimmy will work with you on them. The figures all have to add up exactly."

"He's the only other person who knows what you're doing?"

"Just the three of us, Jack. We have to be careful. No talk to anyone about this."

❈ ❈ ❈ ❈ ❈

By the end of the first year Tony and Jack had large amounts of Rhodesian dollars used to pay their suppliers in cash. In fact, all their creditors were paid in cash.

"We've got too much cash, Tony. I don't know where to put it any longer."

"We'll start creating fictitious invoices, Jack. Jimmy's already got that sorted out. He didn't get a degree in creative accounting for nothing."

"I know he's the best accountant in the country but we've only been doing this for a year and we're already struggling to hide the cash. It's going to keep growing. What's he going to do?"

"Jeez, Jack, I wish you'd stop worrying."

Tony started a book of fictitious retailers. He could bank cash deposits against these false invoices. He derived the greatest pleasure from making OK Bazaars his biggest fictitious customer. They were one of the largest retail groups in southern Africa and Tony had refused to do business with them since the day their buyer had asked Ken Young for a kickback. Meyerton Industries billed them for large amounts of goods for which they always paid in cash.

Chapter Eighteen

The year was 1978.

"I've never been to Hong Kong, Tony. Let's go there on holiday, see what it's like."

"Why not, Renée? I'll organize for us to go after the next trip to Johannesburg."

"That'll be great. We can do some shopping, see the sights."

"We'll go and see Colin, you know, Johnny and Carol Wilson's son. He lives there."

"I'll phone Carol and see if there's anything we can take over for him."

"He's doing very well for himself. He buys diamonds from Mervin. Merv says he keeps talking about this plane he's going to buy."

Tony and Renée arrived in Hong Kong and checked into their hotel. They relaxed for a couple of days, lay by the pool, walked in the nearby streets, window-shopping. Then Tony phoned Colin.

"Hey, Tony, get checked out of that hotel. I'm coming to pick you up. You come stay with me."

Colin's penthouse in Victoria overlooked the harbour. From the western windows Victoria Peak towered against the sky. Colin took them to his roof garden for drinks before dinner.

"I have an old Chinese couple who look after me. He's the best cook in the district. He's making his local specialty for us tonight."

"You've really sorted yourself out, Colin."

"I've been here six years now. Wouldn't live anywhere else."

"I love the local art. I saw some paintings in the street. I want to take some back for my house."

"I'll take you to the factory, Renée. You can pick them up for a song."

"Maybe we'll take some back to Rhodesia to sell to our friends. There's nothing available over there any longer."

"Sanctions really killed the market for luxury items."

"My dad tells me your businesses are doing very well, Tony."

"Yes, we're happy."

"Are you still in the currency trade?"

"That's doing well too."

"Then you might be interested in helping me out?"

"Sure, Colin whatever I can do."

"I want Rhodesian dollars here. Used bank notes."

"How much do you want?"

"As much as you can get out of the country. I'll give you the names of three pilots who'll fly them here from Johannesburg."

"What's the deal?"

"You get them to the pilots in Johannesburg. I'll deposit US dollars in a bank account in Switzerland. You'll get the bank rate."

"We've got ourselves a deal, Colin."

In March of 1978, Ian Smith signed the Salisbury Agreement, an internal settlement designed to introduce a democratic society, free of racial discrimination. Despite the optimism of the politicians, Tony returned to a Rhodesia where war was spreading, prices were rising and morale was plummeting.

He talked to Jack about his meeting with Colin.

"We've got an outlet for all the dollars we're accumulating."

"Thank God, Tony. I haven't got room to hide them any more."

"You know what this means, Jack? There's no limit to the amount of foreign money we can sell to Rhodesians."

"Just keep me out of it as much as possible, Tony."

"I spoke to Dave Miller. He's moved more stuff around southern Africa than anyone."

"When the trucks come up from Johannesburg, I've also got a small shipment of Chinese paintings."

"What are we going to do with those?"

"I want a couple for my house. You can choose what you want. The rest we'll put in our displays in the showroom."

"What sort of profit are we looking at?"

"I paid eight dollars for the small ones. We'll put those up at two hundred dollars."

"What are our costs?"

"No costs except purchase price. They're duty free. We don't even need an import permit."

"Could be a little money spinner, Tony."

"That's what I thought. If they sell well, we'll go back for more."

Tony and Renée took a trip to Hong Kong every few months to choose more Chinese art. The paintings were popular and graced offices, hotels and guesthouses as well as private homes.

They saw Colin Wilson on every trip. He and Tony discussed

business over lunch and, when they parted, he would remind Tony that he would take every Rhodesian dollar that Tony could get out of the country.

Tony sat in his office thinking of ways to shift more dollars to Johannesburg. He went for a walk around the factory and watched the processes of furniture manufacturing. He walked into the showroom and looked at the displays. Then he went to Jack's office, sat opposite Jack and pulled his notepad out of his pocket.

"Give me a pen, Jack. I've just had an idea."

Q: Why did they want used Rhodesian bank notes out of Rhodesia? I thought the currency had no value abroad?

A: It didn't. You couldn't use it outside the country; you couldn't even change it in a bank.

Q: So why did all these people want to take it out?

A: *Tony laughs*. It was funding the war.

Q: Okay … no, actually, I don't understand.

A: There were thousands of terrorists—well, we called them terrorists—they called themselves freedom fighters. Either way, they were trained in the Soviet Union, East Germany, Zambia, Tanzania, Mozambique. They were coming over the border every day. They had to have local money, to live, to blend in.

Q: Did you know this at the time?

A: Of course. We were heading for a black government; the black leaders were waiting to take over. I probably funded them too.

Q: But your friends were being blown up, your sons were fighting in the bush. You were giving your enemies the means to defeat you.

A: I took the opportunity. I don't pretend to be a nice guy.

Q: You once said you'd do anything, legal or illegal, to make money, as long as you don't get caught.

A: *Tony's lips twist into an awkward smile, more of a grimace.* Selling my country and friends down the river. Now you know what a shit I am.

Chapter
Nineteen

// Tony, it's Mervin. I need to see you, old boy."

"Hey, Merv, where've you been? Haven't heard from you in a while."

"Yeah, been around, not here, Mauritius. Can I come to the office?"

Mervin had gained a bit of weight since Tony had last seen him. His face had filled out, his cheeks were plump and shiny and his eyes gleamed behind round glasses. His hair was very short. He looked like a naughty schoolboy. He wore a white T-shirt with 'SEX MACHINE' emblazoned across the chest. It was tucked into khaki bush shorts. He pumped Tony's hand, beaming happily.

"Tony, my old friend, how are you? Good to see you, good to see you."

"What can I do for you Merv?"

"Well, it's a bit delicate, the way things are at the moment. Bit embarrassing, you might say."

"I'll see if I can help."

"I need to borrow some money. Not a lot, but I do need a loan."

"Sorry, Merv, I never lend to a friend."

"I'm in a bind, Tony. I'd never come to you if it weren't serious. You know that. You know I wouldn't."

"I didn't say I wouldn't help. I just said I wouldn't lend you money."

"Are you offering me a job? Is that what you have in mind, old boy?"

"Sort of. Some people I know want to buy uncut diamonds. Perhaps I can set up a meeting."

"How much do they want to spend? Yes, how much money have they got? And what sort of diamonds are they looking for? Uncut diamonds? Polished stones? I can do that, yes sir."

"I don't know. I don't have anything to do with diamonds. I just said I'd send them in the right direction. Let me give them a call."

Tony phoned the Naidoos.

"Ismail, it's Tony. Do you want rough or cut? And how much have you got to spend?"

Tony listened, turned to Mervin.

"What's cheaper?"

"Ismail, rough's about quarter of the price cut … Okay, I'll get back to you."

"Okay, Merv, they want rough diamonds and they've got six million to spend. Can you set it up?"

A few days later Tony and Mervin had lunch together. They met at Friar Tuck's. Tony was a good patron and the owner showed his appreciation by giving them the best table and sending his best waiter to serve them. They ordered the house speciality—thick steaks seared on the grill, basted with a secret barbeque sauce. The chips were fried to perfection and jostled for room with battered onion rings. A large green salad with Roquefort dressing was placed on the table between them. Mervin loaded his plate, added Thousand Island to the Roquefort dressing and twirled the salad with his fork. He took a large mouthful, chewed slowly. He swallowed and looked at Tony.

"The bad news is that I can't get my hands on rough diamonds. I'm not in the rough diamond trade. No, I wish I was, but there you go. I've got an idea, though. Yes, thought about it a lot and I think it's good. If you want to make a lot of money, that is. It's a small sting I have in mind. If you're interested, that is. Maybe it's payoff time after all these years."

"That's forgotten, Merv. But I'm in the money trade. So tell me."

"Well, we'll give them stuff that looks like diamonds. Yes, I'm good at that. They'll never tell the difference. And we'll split the money. It's a lot of money, Tony, yes, could be."

"Beautiful, Merv, let's go for it. And just to sweeten the deal for them I'll put in a million of my own."

Mervin and his partner spent a month in South Africa, creating rough 'diamonds' of different sizes They included two real rough diamonds of good quality. Tony set up the sting in Bulawayo. First he had to get the Naidoos to bite on the deal and willingly part with a lot of money. They were no fools. He called them from his office.

"Ishmail, I'm not having much luck getting these diamonds, but, in my negotiations I've come across a bloke from Angola, who deals in diamonds and is prepared to take the chance of bringing rough stones into the country for you."

"But you don't know this man."

"No, I don't. But I've asked my friend in Johannesburg if he will come and value the stones so you don't get ripped off."

"Okay, Tony. It's more complicated than we hoped, there are more people involved and everyone's going to want paying. I leave that all up to you."

"How much do I get out of this, Ishmail?"

"We send the stones to our family in Bombay where they'll be cut and sold. You'll get ten per cent of what we sell them for."

"Fantastic. In fact, I might even invest a million of my own money."

"We have no problem with that. You come in on one fifth share."

"Great. It's a deal."

Tony called his friend Claude. Claude lived in Victoria Falls. He had left France years before but had never bothered to learn English properly. He enjoyed speaking a broken, 'just left home' sort of English which allowed him to listen in to conversations when people were sure he couldn't understand. He was enthusiastic about his part in the deal.

On Monday the Naidoos arrived early. The younger brother stationed himself at the window, declining coffee. When Mervin and his partner, Errol arrived, Tony introduced them to the Naidoos while they all waited for the Angolan diamond dealer. Claude arrived twenty minutes late, complaining about traffic and missing street signs. He had a false beard and moustache and had dyed his hair dark brown to match. He looked like he should be setting up his easel in Montmartre. Tony introduced him to everyone as Jean-Pierre from Angola. Claude began talking of Angola with a knowledge and passion that was captivating. Tony felt the atmosphere lighten and soften.

"Okay, Jean-Pierre, let's get down to business. Mervin and Errol are going to sort, grade and catalogue every stone. Then they can give the Naidoos a valuation. While they do that the Naidoos can take a couple of diamonds to a gemologist for verification."

"I go for other beeziness. I come later, no?"

"That's fine. Everything is safe here."

Claude handed a cloth bag to Tony and left in a cloud of Gallic gestures. Tony took the bag to his desk and waited for Merv to spread a cotton towel over the surface. He gently tipped the bag and watched the stones tumble onto the cloth. Mervin spread the stones on the desk.

"Ummm, beautiful, these are beautiful."

He picked two small genuine diamonds, put them back in the bag and handed it to Ishmail.

"See what your gemologist says about the quality. It's going to take us some time to go through this lot. We'll be at it most of the day."

❀❀❀❀❀

The Naidoos returned after lunch. They were pleased with what their expert had said and keen to get on with the deal. Mervin and Errol were almost finished.

"I reckon there's about six or seven million dollars-worth of diamonds here, Mr Naidoo."

"We've only got five million."

"Plus my million. Don't worry Ishmail, let me handle Jean-Pierre."

When Jean-Pierre returned Tony led him to the desk. He pulled up a chair for him.

"So 'ow much is eet worth?"

"That is nothing to do with you. How much do you want for the diamonds?"

"My price ees six-and-a-half million."

"The investors only have six million."

"Well, I bring a leetle more. I don' know what your man will value."

"Are you prepared to take six million?"

"Well, okay, but no commission for you."

"Fine, Ishmail, do we have a deal?"

"Yes, we're happy."

"We'll have to pay Mervin a commission when they're sold."

"That's no problem."

Mervin and Errol shook hands all round.

"We have a flight to catch. We must go now."

They closed the door behind them. Ishmail Naidoo placed the bag in his own attaché case, now heavy with money.

At six that evening, Mervin, Errol and Claude arrived at Tony's house. They went through to the verandah, settled in their chairs, accepted drinks from Tony. The sun cast a fiery glow across the sky. The African reds were mirrored in the swimming pool, a giant modern mosaic framed in brick. The scent of Star Jasmine perfumed the air. Mervin stood, extended his glass. The honey-coloured whisky sloshed over the rim.

"Happy days, old boy. Oh, yes, happy days."

Glasses clinked to a chorus of accord.

"Jeez, what a sweet deal."

"It worked just fine."

Claude put the attaché case on the table. Tony pulled his chair up close and opened the case. The money was wrapped in elastic bands, packed tightly. Older, worn notes, creased and dirty, bundled with crisper, fresh ones. Tony laid it on the table in five neat stacks.

"Okay, that's the million I put in. Let's sort out the rest. That's half a million for Claude. Happy, boytjie?"

"Ze best fun ever and now I am ze rich kid."

"Don't spend it all at once."

"Non, non, I 'ide eet from my girlfriend. She spend eet all at once."

"Merv, here's one point five for you, the same for Errol and the same for me."

"Can you change this to rands for us, Tony? Rhodesian dollars are very nice here, yes, nice here, but like bacon at a barmitzvah in Johannesburg."

"Sure, Merv but you'll have to take the going rate."

"Yes, well, of course. What's it these days, old boy?"

"A third of the value, as always."

"Can't complain, can we, Errol. Five hundred thousand rand each, eh? Better than a kick in the pants. Thanks, old boy, appreciate you helping us out."

❀❀❀❀❀

Two months later Tony got a call from Ishmail Naidoo.

"There's a problem. Those aren't diamonds, they're crystal quartz."

"Impossible, Ishmail. Guaranteed impossible."

"Our family says they are not diamonds."

"Jeez, can you trust these people in Bombay?"

"They're our relatives."

"Well, your relatives have just lost me a million dollars."

"We have lost five million, Tony."

"Those blokes from Johannesburg are experts. They'd never make a mistake. You can go down there and they'll show you other stones. I tell you, your relatives are trying to rip us off."

"They cannot do that. They're our relatives."

"But you took some of the stones to be checked here. I think your relatives are crooking you. And if they're crooking you, they're crooking me too."

"They wouldn't do that."

"I've got a million invested in this deal, Ishmail. I've made no commission; my friends in Jo'burg have made nothing. You must find that Frenchman from Angola. You must go to the police."

Chapter
Twenty

Tony's call-up papers arrived in the post in October 1978. He was forty-four years old, a busy and successful businessman in the early years of his second marriage and he didn't want this disruption in his life. He told Renée when he got home that night."

"I have to report for service duty next week, Renée."

"Can't you get out of it, Tony?"

"It's almost impossible to get an exemption. They've started this new call-up system. We all have to do two weeks. They say everyone can take two weeks from their job."

"Where are they sending you for training?"

"I have to report to Brady Barracks."

Sergeant-Major Reynolds was a strong, stocky Englishman. He had been in the military all his life. He'd joined the British army, served in Aden and had discovered a liking for heat and dust. He'd chosen Rhodesia as his new homeland after a chance conversation with a homesick Rhodesian student in a London pub. He joined the Rhodesian Security Forces and became a sergeant-major.

He walked along the line of new recruits standing in the heat of another cloudless day. Shapeless bodies and hung-over faces did not appeal to him. He growled in his throat, turned at the end of the line and planted himself in front of the row of wilting men.

"Each one of you will return home for a haircut. When you appear before me tomorrow you will sport a short-back-and-sides—army fashion. You, you and you will remove your beards and will appear clean-shaven before me tomorrow. Now get out of my sight."

Tony drove home.

"I have to cut off my hair and shave my beard, Renée."

"This whole thing is a joke, Tony. What the hell is happening in this bloody country that they're calling up people like you? And then treating you like kids. We'll see about this."

Renée called up a friend of hers. He was a psychiatrist.

"I'll write him a letter, Renée. Come and pick it up later."

She put down the phone and turned to Tony.

"Guess what? You're a schizophrenic under the care of Doctor Lewis. He's writing a letter to say that he won't be responsible for your behaviour in the event of you having your hair and beard removed. Let the sergeant-major put that in his pipe and smoke it."

Tony returned to Brady Barracks the next day. He lined up with the other men, waiting for Sergeant-Major Reynolds. After twenty minutes, the sergeant-major came down the steps of the building and strode over to the men. He walked down the line, inspecting each man, his face rigid with objection. He drew level with Tony and stopped.

"Do you find it hard to understand simple instructions or are you just a moron?"

Tony reached into his pocket and handed the doctor's letter to Sergeant-Major Reynolds. The man opened it and read it. He eyed Tony; a small smile thinned his lips.

"You need special treatment? I'll see that you get it."

An army truck stopped in front of the men. The driver came over to Sergeant-Major Reynolds and saluted. His dress was faultless.

"Take these men to Kezi, Corporal. Tell the camp commander that the man with the hair is a special case. He'll know what I mean."

The farming district of Kezi lies about a hundred and twenty kilometres south of Bulawayo. In the thick, dry and dusty bush was the training camp, isolated and with few amenities. Men were sent there to learn to follow instructions, to use weapons, to defend their country at all costs.

The new recruits lined up to receive their billeting instructions. The camp commander stood in the shade of an open tent and Tony watched the driver walk over to speak to him, and then salute smartly and return to his vehicle. The commander walked down to the new intake. He stopped in front of Tony.

"Get your hair cut and report back to me."

Tony took the letter from his pocket and handed it to the commander. The man read it, folded it and dropped in on the ground at Tony's feet.

"When the others go for training you will stay with the sergeant. He has work for you."

He pointed to the young coloured man who was standing with the billet forms.

Sergeant Mohammed instructed the new intake to take their kit to their tents and return to him in an hour.

When the other trainees went off to learn the mechanics of war, Sergeant Mohammed took Tony a few hundred metres into the bush. He gave him a shovel and a pile of Hessian sacks.

"Fill them with sand."

The sergeant went and sat under a tree. He took out a book and began to read. Tony made sandbags. The sergeant went off for some coffee then returned to his tree and had a rest. Tony made sandbags. When the sun began to set the sergeant looked at his watch.

"That's it for today."

Tony sat in the small mess hall eating supper. His back ached, his neck felt raw from the sun; he wanted rest and a comfortable bed.

The next morning he watched the other men double-march off to training. Sergeant Mohammed walked with him back to the sandbag area.

"Why're they doing this to you, man?"

"I'm schizo, I go crazy if they cut off my hair. I suppose this is their punishment."

"Just take it easy today."

Tony worked steadily while the sergeant sat under the tree. At ten o' clock the sergeant stopped him.

"Sit in the shade, drink water. Don't kill yourself, man."

"Thanks, Sarge."

Tony sat down next to the sergeant. He drank from the canteen of water.

"What d'you do, what's your job, man?"

"I own some factories. We make furniture, kitchens."

"Can I get a job with you when this is all finished?"

"Sure you can. Just ask for me at Meyerton Industries in Bulawayo."

The sergeant stood up.

"I think we could use some coffee. Stay here, man."

Tony never filled another sandbag. Every day he and the sergeant went into the bush with the shovel and the Hessian bags. They sat under the tree and talked. They drank coffee and played cards. They did push-ups and sit-ups and walked in the bush. Every afternoon the sergeant polished their boots for inspection the next morning.

When Tony's two weeks were up he shook hands with Sergeant Mohammed.

"Come and see me when you're ready. I need people like you."

When Tony returned home he knew he would be called up again.

He put in for exemption, citing his business commitments, pointing out that he couldn't continue exporting to bring in desperately needed foreign currency if he was being sent away every few weeks.

But to no avail. When his next set of call-up papers arrived he found he was assigned to the home guard. He would be protecting the local TV station. His orders were for alternate six-week spells. The television station had been built on top of a hill just outside Bulawayo. It was surrounded by a diamond-mesh fence and the home guard patrolled the perimeter at night. Tony shared the six-to-six shift with two other men.

Tony walked around his station on his first shift. A few lights showed from the buildings but did not light the rough pathway around the fence. He stumbled on rocks and tufts of grass. He realized that if terrorists wanted to blow up the TV station the home guard was no deterrent at all.

Tony went home and rose early the next morning. He sorted out four of the big tennis court lights he used for his photography. He made transportable stands for them and he packed the equipment in his car and went to the factory. In the afternoon he drove to the station and installed a light on each corner of the wire fence. He ran electrical cables from each light back to the guard hut that stood at the entrance to the compound.

That night when he turned on the power the whole fenced-off installation was brilliantly lit up. His fellow patrollers were happy to give Tony the first shift.

"We can sit in here and watch TV and see anyone who might try to approach the station. No terrs are going to get by us."

Tony went off duty at ten and got in his car. He sat in the darkness for a while then leaned forward and turned on the ignition. He headed out of Bulawayo on the main road to Salisbury. The road ran past Brady Barracks.

Tony slowed the car, then U-turned and stopped. He switched off the headlights and waited for his eyes to adjust to the darkness of the street. The main airfield and base on the far side of the road was brightly lit but quiet. On his side of the road was the regular army housing, small government dwellings built many years before. Tony had been here during the day and he knew which house he was interested in. He settled down to wait. At the end of the every evening shift Tony drove out to Brady Barracks. He sat in his car in the unlit street and learned the movements of the occupant of the house opposite the army base. The man was single and lived an unvaried existence. He drank at the base until about eleven then stumbled across the road to his house each night.

On the first Friday of the new month Tony left the TV station at his usual time. He headed down the road and stopped his car at a lay-by. He changed into black trousers and a long-sleeved black shirt. From under the seat he took a balaclava and a pair of black leather gloves. He laid them on the passenger seat. Then he drove to Brady Barracks.

He parked in his usual place a few hundred yards from the man's house. He put on the balaclava and gloves. He felt for the pickaxe handle that protruded from under his seat. He looked at his watch. It was hard to distinguish the time in the pitch-black night but he thought it should be about eleven. He opened his door. Closed it quietly behind him. He walked to the house and stood against a tree outside the garden. It was new moon and the blackness was hardly penetrated by the lights across the road.

He heard the whistling as the man walked along the street. He was bang on time as usual. Tony stood behind the tree holding the pickaxe handle in both hands.

The man passed him and Tony stepped out behind him. He brought the hefty wooden handle down across the man's back. The man dropped to his knees, making a small sound as the air escaped between his teeth. Tony hit him again and the man crumpled unconscious on the pavement.

Tony stood still and listened. All was quiet. He turned the man onto his stomach and pulled his left arm across his back. Then he hit him on the elbow with the pickaxe handle. The bone crunched softly and the arm fell alongside the man's body. Tony laid the other arm across the man's back and hit that elbow with the pickaxe handle. The bone crunched and crumbled under the force of the wooden weapon.

Tony turned and walked to his car. He drove home.

The hospital in Bulawayo tried their best for Sergeant-Major Reynolds. After three months he was loaded in a wheelchair and flown back to England. The NHS embarked on a series of operations in an attempt to repair his broken limbs. They had little result.

Q: That was a horrific thing that you did.

A: That wasn't my last run-in with army types—never could handle these bully-types who thought they could treat people like shit just because they had some authority.

Q: You mentioned before you had a run-in with some colonel or someone?

A: It was one Easter, I was with Renée at the time and we were heading back to Rhodesia after spending the long weekend in South Africa. Being the holiday season we were sitting bumper to bumper, in a fifteen-kilometre queue from the border at Beit Bridge. There were delays at Customs on both sides; it was taking hours to get through. Next thing, a car comes driving on the right-hand side of the road, going against the traffic to try and jump the queue. I thought, 'To hell with you, you can't do this.' I leapt out of the car and a few other drivers joined me and we formed a barrier. It was a fancy Jaguar with a chauffeur, so I knew it was probably some top brass sitting at the back. I shouted at them and told them to get back in the queue; we had all been waiting for hours. The driver ignored us and kept inching forward; although there were eight of us we couldn't stop the car. I just thought 'Fuck you, I don't care who you are, you don't go and break the law.' I picked up a rock and bashed in both headlights. I yelled at the driver, 'Before I fucking break your window go to the back of the queue!' and he did.

Q: More violence?

A: But then about a week later I had a visit from two CID guys. They arrived at the factory and wanted to charge me for assaulting the vice president of Rhodesia, Colonel Everard. I yelled at them, 'I don't care who the fuck he is; he has no right to break the laws of another country; he should at least respect the laws of South Africa and not drive on the wrong side of the road to try to jump the queue. If you don't fuck off right now I'll go to the papers.' Well, that was the end of that—end of story!

Chapter
Twenty-one

// My name's Jaco du Plessis. I'm a friend of Dave Miller."

"Dave's a good guy. What can I do for you, Jaco?"

"I want Rhodesian dollars in South Africa."

"I can give you South African rands"

"No, Tony, must be dollars."

"I'd be taking a hell of a risk. Exchange control is very strict."

"Cash notes, and no official documents. You'll be paid well."

"How well?"

"I want fifty thousand dollars initially. You'll get the equivalent in rands."

"That's a good deal. I think the rate's about sixty-six cents to the dollar at the moment. Let me see what I can do."

Tony showed Jaco out, then stood at his office window, looking out onto the factory floor. The hum of machinery didn't enter his consciousness; he didn't notice the activity of the blue-overalled workers. He thought about Dave Miller. Dave lived in Botswana. He was a languid Englishman who had taken Africa as his.

Tony and Dave had been working together for months now. Tony supplied him with Rhodesian dollars. Dave got the dollars to Switzerland where they were exchanged at the bank rate for US dollars. The money went into Tony's Swiss bank account and he then sold them to Rhodesians who wanted money out of the country. He was making a nice packet on the deals. He could be making more. There were a lot of payoffs involved—the pilots who flew the Rhodesian dollars to Mozambique, the shippers who took them to Hong Kong.

Tony walked across to his desk. He picked up the telephone, pressed a button. He could see into his partner's office through the big window. He watched Jack pick up his telephone.

"Are we working late tonight, Jack?"

"I think we've got our twelve sets for this week."

"I'd like to make a couple more."

"Okay. I can stay till seven."

Tony tilted back the chair, smelled the warm leather. The inlay on the big desk was the same rich burgundy, tooled with gold around the edges. The desk was neat; papers arranged precisely, three telephones in a straight row. Tony and Jack employed a large administration staff; the factory ran like clockwork. The staff was loyal and hardworking. Their monthly cheques reflected half their salaries, keeping them in a lower tax bracket; the other half was paid in cash.

The staff left at five and Tony locked the showroom doors. Jack was already machining the pine boards when Tony returned to the factory floor. Within an hour an extra pair of bedside cabinets stood with the other twelve. Every week this special order was loaded on the trucks with the rest of the export goods for South Africa. The pine cabinets that Tony and Jack manufactured after hours looked identical to the ones made daily in the factory. Only a psychic could have known that the special cabinets were made with a false floor and that hundreds of used Rhodesian bank notes left the country concealed in this hidey-hole. When Jack left, Tony coded the cabinets with prepared stickers and loaded the bottoms with twenty-five thousand dollars each. Then he switched off the lights and locked up behind him.

Tony and Renée went to Johannesburg every month. Sometimes they took the camper and stopped off along the way, making the trip into a mini-holiday. They would always stay a night or two with Mom and then move to their twelfth-floor flat in Hillbrow. It overlooked the park and they loved to sit in the enclosed balcony to enjoy their evening drink. Hillbrow was full of young, vibrant people. It was also convenient to Selby where the special orders from Rhodesia were stored until Tony's next visit to Johannesburg.

Tony and Renée had been in Johannesburg for two days. He had been to the storeroom in Selby and sorted the latest order of bedside cabinets. The meeting with Jaco was scheduled for three o' clock. They would conclude the dollar/rand exchange. Tony waited on the couch in the living room. He watched a video from his extensive collection. Renée was on the balcony, looking through a magazine but very aware of the large sum of money in the cupboard to her right. When the doorbell rang she settled back in her chair and became absorbed in an article on couture fashion.

Jaco stepped into the flat. He shook Tony's hand stiffly.

"You've got the money, Tony?"

"All fifty thou."

"Can I see it?"

"Sure, come through."

Jaco followed Tony onto the balcony. He nodded at Renée then bent to see the money stacked on the bottom shelf of the cupboard.

"Okay, Tony, my partner will be here at two 'o clock tomorrow with the rands."

"I only want used notes, Jaco. If you bring new notes, the deal's off."

Tony watched Jaco get in the lift. He closed the door and went into the tiny kitchen. He rested his hands on the counter and stared at the glass-fronted cupboards. His reflection stared back at him with unseeing eyes. The clock above the stove ticked steadily. Renée called from the balcony and he opened the cupboard and took down two glasses. He took the drinks outside and handed one to Renée. He pulled his chair close to hers, sat down and rested his arm along her shoulders.

"There's something not right, Renée. Why didn't he bring the money with him?"

"He doesn't know you, Tony. Maybe he wanted to make sure you weren't setting him up."

"This is like '73. That Swiss deal. Now he's got a partner involved. I don't like it."

"Well, let's be careful."

"Stay on the balcony all the time tomorrow then, if I have to shoot the bastard, I'll know where you are."

When the doorbell rang at two the next day, Renée was reading in her chair on the balcony. Tony opened the door to a tall, dark-haired man who introduced himself as Hennie Coetzee. He spoke with a strong South African accent and wore a light-coloured suit without a tie. His handshake was firm. He walked into the flat and put his briefcase on the table, bending to open it.

"I've got your rands, Mr Meyer."

"But these are all new notes, Mr Coetzee. I won't take new notes."

"Jaco didn't tell me that. I can assure you it's all here, Mr Meyer."

"I don't think you heard me, Mr Coetzee. I won't take new notes."

"Let me go and speak to Jaco. I'll be back soon with used notes."

Tony locked the door and turned to see Renée watching the street from the balcony.

"There are three other blokes down there and Coetzee has just got into the car with them."

"They're trying to set me up."

"They look like cops, Tony. Pack the money in a plastic bag and bring it into the bedroom."

"We can't hide it in the flat."

"No, but we can't hide it outside either. Bring it to me in the bedroom."

When Tony came into the bedroom Renée had a hatbox on the bed. She positioned the money on her head and fixed it with hairpins, then covered the packet with a turban-styled hat from the hatbox. Her blond hair curled from under the hat and she looked very fashionable as she applied thick eyelashes and a coat of lipstick.

"I'll be in the coffee shop on the corner. I'll call you in a couple of hours."

❁❁❁❁❁

Two hours later Renée listened to Tony on the telephone.

"Coetzee came back with two other blokes. They wanted to see the money."

"What did you say?"

"I told them the money wasn't here. I took them onto the balcony and opened the cupboard for them."

"They must have been a bit surprised."

"They said that we were meant to do a deal and wanted to know why the money wasn't here. I told them I'd got a funny feeling this morning and had taken it to a friend's house."

"Did they believe you?"

"I think so. We've set it up for tomorrow morning. I'll have the dollars and they'll have the used notes."

"Are you going to do the deal?"

"No, it's a set-up. Stay there. I'll come pick you up. We'll go to Mom's."

Mom was busy in the kitchen when they arrived. She was making a fruit trifle to go in her fridge. Her fridge was full of prepared dishes which she could pull out for Tony and Renée at a moment's notice.

"Can we stay tonight, Mom?"

"You have to ask? Your room is always ready."

"I have to make a couple of calls. Then we can have a drink on the stoep."

Tony went into the study. He closed the door gently and sat at the desk. This was his South African workplace; he had everything he needed to carry on his business. He unlocked the desk drawer and took out a well-used telephone directory. He dialled Rhodesian Customs in Bulawayo.

" I need to speak to Kevin Miles."

"Chief Inspector Miles."

"Hello, Kevin. It's Tony Meyer. I've got a funny situation down here. Some bloke has approached me. He wants to give me rands for Rhodesian dollars. He's talking a lot of money. How can I trap him?"

"We'll set it up for next time you go down, Tony. We'll give you dollars to take with you and get Commercial Branch in Johannesburg involved. We'll give them a cut."

"Thanks very much, Kevin. I'll see you when I get back."

The following morning Tony was up early. He laid the dollars out on the desk and started to cut paper to the same size as the bank notes. He put a genuine note on the top and bottom of each pile and secured it with an elastic band. When he was finished he packed them together and stood back to look at the piles of false money. A casual look would not reveal that this was not a large amount of used bank notes. He put them in a carry bag and went to his car.

The drive into Johannesburg took him through the suburbs of his youth and he arrived at Marshall Square in a good mood. He took the bag, locked the car and went up the stairs to the front desk of Police Headquarters in Johannesburg. He asked for the head of Commercial Branch and was directed down a brightly lit corridor to a large office at the end. He introduced himself to the florid man behind the desk.

"I'm involved with Rhodesian Customs. We're trying to trap a man setting up deals here in Johannesburg to buy Rhodesian dollars."

"I'm going to send you downstairs, Mr Meyer. I have a special section that is only involved with currency deals."

Tony followed the directions to an office at the back of the building on the ground floor. The corridor walls were painted dark brown to hip height and thick cream to the ceiling and smelled of sweat and old coffee. He stepped round a large black woman polishing the floor with a rag she dipped in a tin of Cobra. At least the floor polish improved the smell a bit, though he suspected that she added daily to the all-pervading stink of body odour.

Tony stopped at the door of the office. A bald man sat at the desk, his finger pointing out a section in the papers in front of him. Leaning over to read the indicated words was Jaco.

"And what are you doing here, Jaco?"

"I could say the same to you."

"I've come to show Commercial Branch how we're setting up the trap for you."

Tony tipped the bag of false money onto the desk. It looked very real as the bundles tumbled across the papers. Jaco picked up a stack and took off the elastic band. He fanned the paper, looked at the real note, turned it to look at the note underneath.

"You're trying to pull the wool over our eyes."

"No, I'm not. I've already alerted Rhodesian Customs. You can phone them and check. Ask for Kevin Miles. Here's his number."

The bald man reached for the telephone.

Chapter
Twenty-two

In April of 1979 Rhodesia elected its first black government. Bishop Abel Muzorewa led the Government of National Unity into office and Zimbabwe–Rhodesia was formally launched on the 1st June. Neither Britain nor America recognized the new government.

Emigration had been running at a rate of about fifteen hundred people a month but slowed to a third of that as people waited and hoped for peace. It was not to be. By July, the war was draining thirty-seven per cent of the national budget. Robert Mugabe's ZANLA forces were attacking the country from their bases in Mozambique to the east and the ZIPRA armies of Joshua Nkomo were raiding from Zambia and Botswana. The Rhodesian Security Forces launched their own cross-border raids intending to destroy the guerrilla bases and halt the tide of infiltration.

Tony arrived back in his office from a late lunch to find a man waiting for him. He introduced himself as Vote Moyo.

"I am Mr Nkomo's commander-in-chief."

Tony asked for coffee to be brought to his office.

"What can I do for you, Mr Moyo?'

"We are looking for donations to buy a warehouse for our goods."

"What sort of goods?"

"The world has given us many things."

"Do you have guns among the things, Mr Moyo?"

"No, these are all things to help the people."

"How much money are you looking for?"

"We want thirty thousand dollars from each businessman. It will be an investment for your future."

Tony looked at the man sitting across from him. He knew just where his future lay. The talk was that Joshua Nkomo would play a big part in it. Would giving the money ensure anything? Would refusing put him in jeopardy? He sipped his coffee.

"I have another idea, Mr Moyo. Come with me."

Tony led the way out of his office and across the busy manufacturing section of the factory. The whine of machinery prevented any exchange of words. They walked to the end of the dispatch area and through open double doors. To the right was the sectioned-off showroom but the rest of the space was a massive area, part stockroom, and part general storage.

"I've twenty thousand square feet of floor area here. Is this big enough for all you want to do?"

Vote Moyo walked forward. He looked around, clasped his hands behind his back and gazed at the steel rafters. He turned back to Tony.

"It will be suitable, Mr Meyer."

"I'll give it to you for six months, Mr Moyo."

"I will send word when the goods arrive."

Towards the end of the year, seven trainloads were trucked to the warehouse. Tony walked among the workers, unloading, packing, piling. He ordered the twenty thousand tons of flour to be packed in the coolest part of the area. He kept the hundred tons of Belgian sugar alongside the flour. Three truckloads of Russian sardines separated the foodstuffs from the collapsible boats and outboard motors, donated for troops to cross the Zambezi River. Piles of thick Russian blankets, too hot for use in the tropics were put to work protecting the delicate Czechoslovakian fine china coffee sets. One hundred and fifty sewing machines and an equal number of knitting machines had been donated by Singer in America.

Tony set aside an area especially for the four-litre plastic containers of Swedish cooking oil. The plastic was looking discoloured and he suspected that it might have been in the sun. He didn't want a river of oil to contend with.

He and Jack marvelled at the boxes of matches. The same lion motif on a yellow background that Rhodesian matches displayed, but all the writing was in Russian. There were enough matches to last the whole country five years. When the workers unpacked three thousand dozen metal files from Poland, Tony had to ask the foreman what on earth they could be for.

"They are different sizes and cuts. See, some are round and these are like triangles."

"Yes, but what are they for?"

"They are for repairing our AK-47s, sir."

Not a single box had ever been opened.

The goods sat in Tony's warehouse. After a few months, the foreman complained to Tony and Jack about weevils in the flour. They went to inspect the flour and found the floor black with the little insects. Tony telephoned Nkomo's office.

"You've got a problem. Your flour is infected with weevils."

"Get the fumigators, Mr Meyer."

"Then you'll have to throw it all away. It'll be poisoned."

"Is there anything you can do?"

"Let me think about it."

Tony walked across to the window. He looked out on the factory floor, watched his staff busy at their jobs. He imagined the great pile of flour in the next room slowly turning black and undulating its way over to his office, taking over the whole building, burying the city. He laughed and turned back to his desk. He would get hold of Benny Lobel.

Lobels were the biggest bakers in Bulawayo. They supplied the city and surrounding areas with government-subsidized brown and white bread, with fancy rolls, French loaves and kitke on Friday.

Benny Lobel arrived a few hours later with his master baker. They all walked around the flour. The baker opened a bag and took a handful of the flour. He caressed it with his fingers, feeling the quality of the soft powder. He opened his hand, blew gently and watched the flour rise up in a white cloud. Then he studied the small mound remaining in his palm. He looked at his boss, shook his head.

"I think you'll have to dump it, Tony."

"It belongs to Joshua Nkomo. Are you willing to tell him to throw it way?"

Lobel sighed heavily and stared at the floor. Then he opened a few more bags. He passed each bag to his baker who gazed at the flour, watching for movement. They stood aside and discussed the situation.

"Okay, Tony. We'll start mixing it in with our good flour. We'll try it for a week and if there are no complaints about the bread we'll continue."

"How much can you pay Nkomo?"

"We'll give him eighty per cent of the price we pay for flour."

Nkomo was pleased that the problem had been resolved.

"The people will be healthy. They will be getting protein in their bread at no extra cost," he boomed with a smile.

In September, Britain convened the Lancaster House Conference. Talks continued for over three months culminating in a signed agreement in December. The ceasefire came into effect at the end of December, sanctions were lifted and the country went to the polls in February 1980.

Robert Mugabe and his ZANU (PF) party won a landslide victory.

Heavy drops of rain pelted the corrugated-iron roof of the factory, adding to the noise of the working machinery. Tony closed his office door against the sound and joined Dave Miller at the coffee table. He added sugar to the steaming mug in front of him and slowly stirred the contents.

"Jeez, Dave, the country's got it coming now."

"Yeah. We were so sure that the Brits would never let a Marxist in."

"There goes my job as the new Minister of Finance."

"Do you think Nkomo would have given you the position, Tony?"

"Who knows? I'd have been bloody good in the job, I'd have made Zimbabwe rich."

"And had a good salary."

"I wouldn't have taken a salary. Commission only, two-and-a-half per cent. Anyway that's out the window now."

"Yeah, unlikely to find something like that again. You got the import permit for Nkomo's matches?"

"Sure, Tony, it came through from Botswana yesterday. I'll organize to pick up the matches next week."

"That'll free me up a bit more space."

Tony watched the rivulets of rain run down the office windows. He sipped his coffee and wondered how much of a liability his relationship with Joshua Nkomo would be in a country now headed by Nkomo's political rival, Robert Mugabe.

✤✤✤✤✤

Q: How well did you know Joshua Nkomo?

A: I got to know him very well. He became a valued customer.

Q: He bought goods from you?

A: Absolutely. I presented him with a big office desk and chair for his new house. But he paid to furnish the house and all the flats, farms and conference centres he acquired.

Q: So the relationship stayed on a business level?

A: I never saw him socially, if that's what you mean. I developed a relationship with Nkomo for expediency. We thought he would come to power.

Q: What happened to all the goods in your factory?

A: A refinery took the Swedish cooking oil. It was rancid by then and they refined it and sold it. They paid Nkomo seventy-five per cent of their net profit.

Q: And there were all those matches?

A: Dave Miller took the matches to Gaborone in Botswana. From there they were sold to Nigeria. The metal files were sold to a hardware wholesaler in Johannesburg. I slowly emptied the factory for him.

Q: What was your cut?

A: Not a penny. I made sure that he got every last cent. I've no idea what he did with the money.

Q: So the people of Zimbabwe never saw any of the goods donated to them by foreign countries. They never benefited at all?

A: You're talking about Africa. The people never benefit.

Chapter
Twenty-three

Robert Mugabe set up his cabinet of twenty-two members of parliament. He included two members from Ian Smith's party and four members of Joshua Nkomo's party. Joshua Nkomo was given the job of Minister of Home Affairs in the new government. He was to create a new national police force out of the three armies that had fought each other for fifteen years.

The euphoria of the new nation dissipated in the wake of unemployment and political rivalry. In November 1980, fighting broke out between ZANU and ZAPU. In January 1981, Nkomo was sacked from his post and offered a lesser portfolio. In February, fighting broke out yet again. The former guerrilla armies were ordered to lay down their arms. Instead they concealed stocks of weapons in secret arms dumps.

Tony's manufacturing businesses continued to provide the retailers with goods and he exported truckloads of furniture to South Africa. Life in the cities remained unaffected by the outbreaks of violence in the army camps but the new political dispensation manifested in other ways, as the government clamped down on any business remotely suspected of supporting ZAPU.

Towards the end of the year Meyerton Industries was subjected to a third visit from the authorities.

Tony fielded the phone call in his office.

"Mr Meyer, my name is Paul Siegel. I'm from the Income Tax Department. We'd like to come and inspect your books."

"Of course, Mr Siegel."

"We'll be there on Tuesday. Please have everything ready for us."

"I shall tell my staff to give you every assistance."

Tony walked over to Jack's office. As he passed the administration section he glanced through the window. He could see their receptionist, Pixie, talking on the telephone. The typists and clerks were busy at their desks. Hilda, the office assistant was bent over a filing cabinet and the dispatch manager was talking to his accountant, Jimmy. The staff were used to disruptions. They had put up with Rhodesian Customs for three months. Customs had examined every export document. They had offloaded trucks to check the manifests. It took a day to load a truck so, for every truck they checked, the company lost two days. Instead of a trip a week, the trucks were down to a trip every two weeks. Tony put more trucks on the road to make up the difference.

Tony knocked on Jack's door and went in. The office was the mirror image of his own but Jack had chosen furniture in a light beech. A dark blue wool rug offset the pale chairs and coffee table at the end of the room.

Jack's vast L-shaped desk was strewn with papers. Two copper ashtrays and an empty coffee cup vied for space on the surface. A *House and Home* magazine lay open over the telephone. Tony stood behind the high-backed visitor's chair and looked at the desk with distaste.

"Jeez, what a mess."

"I'm doing costings for the new range, Tony."

"In this mess? Only a fool would believe that."

"I'll get Hilda to bring us coffee, Tony. Then I'll show you."

Jack closed the magazine. He opened a drawer—the space was already filled with newspapers and periodicals and he forced the pile of paper down, laid the magazine on top and closed the drawer again. He took a deep drag on the cigarette smouldering in the ashtray then placed it back on the stubs already there. He stacked the mess of papers and placed them on the short L of the desk, holding them with the coffee cup. Hilda knocked and brought in a tray, which she put on the desk between them. She took the empty cup and left. A faint trace of soap lingered and disappeared, overpowered by the smell of tobacco. Tony walked to the air-conditioner and turned it to high.

"You know I hate air-conditioning."

"Well, if you want to smoke, Jack, you have to keep it on. You can hardly breathe in here."

"I'd rather keep the windows open."

"You've been in here for an hour and they're still closed."

"I was busy, I forgot."

Tony sat down in the chair and leaned forward over the desk.

"Let's look at the costings."

Jack isolated a sheaf of papers and pushed them toward Tony.

"These sheets are in inches and those are the millimetre ones."

"These are the straight conversions, Jack?"

"Yes. The reduced conversions are done in black."

Tony looked at each sheet of paper. He placed them together and handed them back to Jack.

"Okay. Get rid of anything that can get us into trouble. We've got away with this so far."

"Sometimes I wonder how you come up with these things."

"I'm just brilliant."

"No doubt about that. I only hope we don't get caught."

"We're about to find out."

"What do you mean, Tony?"

"Mr Paul Siegel of the tax department is going to pay us a visit."

"Oh, shit, what does he want?"

"He wants to check our books."

"But we've just been checked by Customs. And the Fraud Squad were here in April. We've had every bloody government department on our backs."

"Calm down, Jack. They might think they smell a rat but they're too fucking stupid to find the carcass."

Paul Siegel and his partner Dennis Smith spent week after week going through the books at Tony's factory. They investigated piles of folders; studied pages of figures; compared bank statements and invoices and export orders.

The administration staff were polite but distant. They resented this intrusion into their lives and this unwarranted 'assault' on their bosses.

One Thursday afternoon there was knock on his door and Paul Siegel entered with a sheaf of papers in his hand.

"There's something I need to clear up here, Mr Meyer."

"Please, sit down, Mr Siegel."

"I have asked your staff about this. They have no idea. Perhaps you can explain."

"I'll try."

"You are selling this article in Rhodesia for two hundred and ten dollars. The same article is being exported at one hundred and forty dollars. Why's that?"

"It's very simple, Mr Siegel. The South African market is very competitive. That's the price that they'll accept."

"I'd like to see your costings, Mr Meyer."

"Those are handled by my partner. I'll ask him to bring them over."

Paul Siegel studied the cost sheets, added figures, made notes in his notebook and asked for the raw material purchase sheets.

Tony sat with Jack at the coffee table. They discussed the new line they were launching.

"Mr Meyer, your gross profit on the local market is thirty-three per cent as opposed to ten per cent on export orders. You could be selling your products much cheaper here."

"But why should I, Mr Siegel?"

Paul Siegel grunted. He folded his arms and looked at the piles of papers on the desk. Tony walked over to him.

"If you would like me to stop exporting please give me a government letter saying so and I will stop immediately."

Paul Siegel raised his hand and rubbed his fingers over his forehead as though smoothing the furrows of his frown. He sighed deeply.

"That will not be necessary, Mr Meyer."

Two weeks later Tony and Jack sat at the bar in the Hotel Victoria. Tony ordered a Coke. He watched the barman pour it over the ice cubes, slice the lemon and add it to the drink. Jack had already started on his double whisky. He pulled deeply on his cigarette, tapped the end on the ashtray and sucked at the smoke again. The cigarette glowed deep red, gained another length of ash. Tony watched the smoke curl towards the ceiling; dissipate in the draught of the fan. The bar was filling with after-work regulars and hummed with the comforting buzz of conversation. Tony smiled at the blonde seated at a nearby table. She smiled back but returned to watch the door. He'd give her awaited companion ten more minutes and then he'd go and join her.

"Thank God the tax people have finished. I don't know how much more I could stand."

"What's with you Jack? They'll never find out how we do it."

"I don't know why we have to do it at all, Tony? We make a good living as it is." Jack looked edgy but Tony had heard it all before.

"Not the same old whine, Jack. You're certainly quiet when you spend the extra money."

"My nerves aren't what they used to be. There's too much going on. All these people being killed, and this new government ..."

"You've never had any nerve, Jack."

Chapter
Twenty-four

In February 1982, Joshua Nkomo was dismissed from the government. In March, five senior ex-ZIPRA officers were arrested and charged with treason. In August, Vote Moyo was arrested. He was detained without trial.

Tony and Renée lay on the loungers in the garden while they relished the peace of Mom's house in Johannesburg.

Tony reached over and stroked Renée's arm. She was oiled for the sun and her skin flowed beneath his fingers, fine pale hairs against the darker background—like an exotic dessert.

Coconut teased his nostrils.

"What day is it?"

"Don't stop. It's Friday, Tony."

"We've been here a week. Must be the eleventh then."

"Umm ... suppose so ... don't stop, feels so good."

"Know what day it is?"

"I just told you, silly."

"No I meant the 11th of November. It's Armistice Day."

"Is it? Do we have to get poppies or something?"

"Don't think so. But it's an important day in our own history."

"Why?"

"It's the day Ian Smith declared UDI."

"I've never been into politics."

"If he hadn't done that seventeen years ago you wouldn't be enjoying a massage from a very rich man."

"The combination of you and money has always been irresistible. Don't stop what you're doing."

"Sorry, but Mom's calling. Be right back."

"I'll be waiting."

Tony walked across the lawn, fine and soft and the green of emeralds. Smudges of colour defined the edges and contrasted with the buff-coloured house. Mom stood in the doorway, silver hair in the sunlight, glasses glinting.

"It's the telephone. It's Jimmy in Bulawayo."

"Thanks Mom. He probably wants to know our flight number. Go sit with Renée, I'll bring drinks when I've finished talking to him."

Tony walked to the study. He sat on the edge of the desk, reached for the phone.

"Hello Jimmy, don't know what to do with yourself when I'm away, hey?"

"Tony, it's serious, very serious. There's a warrant out for your arrest. You're accused of spying for South Africa ... treason."

Tony laid the phone back in its cradle. He walked over to the window and looked out at the basking garden, in the sun. He could see Mom sitting on a chair and Renée leaning towards her. The shadows of the trees reached across the grass and he looked at his watch. It was almost four o'clock.

Tony walked to the desk and sat down in the chair. He picked up the air tickets that lay on the blotter. They had been due to fly back to Bulawayo on Sunday.

The door opened and Renée came into the room.

"You're taking such a long time."

"I'm in big shit, Renée. There's a warrant out for my arrest."

"For Christ's sake, what's going on up there? Have they gone quiet mad?"

"We can't go back. You know what's happening to people in prison."

"How much do they know?"

"They don't know anything. They're accusing me of treason."

"Treason? Why? Why treason?"

"Who knows, Renée. They say I've been spying for South Africa."

"That's a joke. They want you on currency, you know they do."

"I don't think it's that. I think it's to do with my association with Nkomo. We can't go back. I've had a good run, made a lot of money. We've got money down here, houses. We'll start again."

"Get me on a flight tomorrow, Tony. I'll take what I want out the house, load it in the camper and take it to the kids."

"It's not safe for you to go."

"It's you they want, Tony. I'll be okay."

Renée sipped her coffee. It was late morning and she still had a lot of things she needed to do. She looked at the list, crossed off one item then wrote down two more. The door of the coffee shop opened and she glanced up at the man who walked in. He smiled at her, came over to the table.

"Hello, Mrs Meyer. I didn't know you were back."

Renée smiled at him. He was a friend of Tony's but she didn't know him well. The man leaned down over the table. He lowered his voice.

"You've got a problem, Mrs Meyer. The police are looking for you. You've got to get out of town. I'll pick you up this evening and get you out through Plumtree."

"Is this necessary, Tommy?"

"Definitely, Mrs Meyer. For Tony I'll do anything."

Tommy straightened, turned to leave. He raised his hand as he went out the door. Renée drank her coffee. She went to the counter to pay and asked to use the telephone. She called Richard.

"I want to have lunch with you Richard."

"I don't know if I can, Mom. I've got meetings all day."

"I want to have lunch, Richard. Pick me up at twelve. Outside the Victoria."

Renée walked down the street. It was almost twelve and she saw Richard's car at the curb.

She got in, closed the door.

"Get me to the airport, Richard. I'm on the next flight to Johannesburg."

When the police arrived at the Meyer's Bulawayo house that evening, Renée was having lamb casserole with Tony and Mom in Johannesburg.

Chapter
Twenty-five

It was 1983.

"Jimmy says you're not coming back, Tony?"

"I can't, Jack. But I'm safe here. There's no extradition agreement between Zimbabwe and South Africa."

"What are you going to do?"

"I'm going to expand the business this end. Just keep it going up there, Jack. Keep exporting. When we've got enough down here and it's up and running then you come down."

"They'll come looking for me, Tony."

Tony heard the tremor in Jack's voice. He clenched his jaw, tried for the right amount of firmness and reassurance.

"Just stay there, Jack. You know nothing about what I was doing. Denounce me; it doesn't matter. Just keep the business for a few more years ... or forever."

✿✿✿✿✿

Four days later Jack called again.

"Tony, I'm at Jan Smuts Airport. Come and get me."

Tony sighed. He found his keys, got in his car and set off for the airport. He drove to the arrivals entrance and saw Jack waiting on the pavement. At his feet was a small suitcase; he looked like he was coming for the weekend stopover.

"Hello, Tony. I'm here."

Tony got out the car, took the suitcase and put it in the boot. Jack grinned, stood where he was. His eyes seemed distant, unfocused. Tony opened the passenger door, took his arm and helped him into the seat.

"What's going on, Jack?"

"I've left, never going back, all mad wogs and Englishmen up there."

He giggled, swayed in his seat.

"What've you been drinking, Jack?"

"Nothing, Tony. Just the medicine the doctor gave me, for my anxiety, you know."

Tony took Jack home to Mom.

"He's on valium, Mom. Let him sleep it off, I'll talk to him tomorrow."

Tony drove to his townhouse in Sandton. He'd bought the three-bedroom duplex in September, Renée had organized the decorators in October and they had stayed there for the first time on their Johannesburg trip in November. It was now their new home. Townhouses were becoming very popular in Johannesburg and new complexes were springing up in all the suburbs. He'd bought another two townhouses in other complexes at the same time. He had paid cash for them all. One belonged to Jack and had been registered in his wife, Lorraine's name. He had registered his own two in Renée's and his daughter's names.

Jack's townhouse had been rented out and Tony was glad that the tenant had signed a short lease. Lorraine was packing up everything in Zimbabwe and would be down by Christmas, things being equal.

Tony and Renée went to Cape Town for Christmas. They needed to lie on the beach at Clifton, walk in the gardens at Kirstenbosch, and take the cable car up Table Mountain. They spent Christmas with friends and family and began enjoying South Africa as their new home.

In January Tony had a call from Jimmy.

"We've just started production again after the Christmas break, Tony."

"Has the warrant of attachment made a difference to you, Jimmy?"

"There's some bloke called Diederichs who has come in here to take over. He's assessed the factory, listed the assets. He says we'll keep our jobs but that we work for the government now."

"It's this new law of Mugabe's, Jimmy."

"Afraid so, Tony. Enemies of the state forfeit everything. They're going to take the lot. I hear they attached your house and possessions."

"Jack's too. The minute he left."

"Yeah. You know Pixie moved in to Jack's house with Herbert Ushuwekunze."

"How the hell did they ever get together? Our one-legged receptionist with Mugabe's Minister of Foreign Affairs."

"She's a real doll, Tony."

"I know, Jimmy, but they're still an unlikely couple."

"What does Jack think about them living in his house?"

"He doesn't care, he's happy for Pixie. He's better since he's been here. A bit like the old Jack I used to know."

"They're paying us all from your bank accounts, Tony. I don't know how long the money will last because they've stopped the export orders."

"Meyerton Industries won't survive without exporting, Jimmy. Better keep your eyes open for something else."

Tony put the phone down, opened his desk drawer and found his telephone book. He opened it, ran his finger down the list of numbers and picked up the phone again. A strong female voice answered on the second ring.

"Palance Shipping and Forwarding."

"Barney Palance, please."

Tony straightened the telephone while he waited, put the pens back in their holder, closed the phone book and returned it to the drawer.

"Hello, Barney, it's Tony Meyer."

"Ah, Tony, yes, your consignment should be here by Wednesday."

Well, Barney, don't allow it to go on to Zimbabwe. I've had a bit of trouble up there and I can't go back. They've attached all my assets and if you send the consignment up you won't get paid. Sell the lot here in South Africa."

"Thanks for letting me know, Tony. I hope you get it sorted out but if you need any help, just shout."

A cousin of Renée's had set up a meeting between Tony and a man named Jerry Davids. Jerry had a wholesale electrical company, which was doing very well. He also had a furniture factory that was doing very badly. Its losses were running at five million rand and Jerry was gatvol subsidizing it through the electrical company. He hadn't been able to sell it and he couldn't liquidate without losing his other business. He thought Tony would be the ideal person to put it right.

"I think it will be a wonderful thing for you, Tony."

"What will be a wonderful thing for me?"

"If you can put my business right."

"No, Jerry. That will be a wonderful thing for you."

"Look Tony, this is what I'll offer. If you can turn it around and start making a profit I'll give you fifty per cent of the business."

"I can't come on my own, Jerry. I handle marketing and sales, my partner does the manufacturing side. The fifty per cent goes to both of us when we get it right."

"How long do you think it will take?"

"Let's take a drive out there. We'll have a look and I'll be able to give you an answer."

Tony picked up Jack and headed out to Babelegi, a government-subsidized industrial area in one of the homelands, a hundred and twenty kilometers north of Johannesburg. Tony and Jack inspected the factory. It was well set up with good machinery, manufacturing a wide range of indoor and garden furniture. Generally it was poorly made. Jack spoke to the foreman, who told him that ninety per cent of the goods were returned to the factory because of bad finishing. The workforce then spent their time trying to improve the finish before sending it back to the retailer.

"We can turn this around quite quickly, Tony. They don't know what they're doing here."

"You're right, Jack. And we'll cut the range in half, concentrate on items we know sell well."

Tony walked over to Jerry.

"We'll turn this around in six months, Jerry. We'll need salaries and a company car each and Jack will need accommodation close by."

"No problem with that. There's a company house in Hammanskraal which he can have."

"We'll start immediately, Jerry. The sooner we turn a profit the sooner we have our own company again."

Tony contacted the South African retailers who had been buying his Zimbabwean export range and, as the orders came, in Jack was ready to put the new items into production. He taught the employees good workmanship and how to finish a piece of furniture and the factory began to produce a smaller range of higher quality goods. For the first time the trucks returned empty from their deliveries.

When Tony and Jack had taken over the company in January it had been running at a loss of ninety thousand rand a month. Four months later, April's month-end figures showed that the business had broken even for the first time. They had a small celebration at the factory and promised the staff a good Christmas bonus if production continued to improve. At the monthly meeting in early May the company accountant declared that the month-end figures would show a profit. Tony called in to see Jerry Davids the following morning.

"The company's now up and running, Jerry. You have April's figures; your accountant says we'll make a profit in May. Please issue Jack and me with our shares."

"Yes, Tony, a deal's a deal. You can have the shares but I can't give you fifty per cent, only forty-nine per cent."

"Well, one per cent doesn't matter to me. I'm not looking to take over. I'm looking for what I deserve out of this."

"I want fifty thousand rand from each of you for your shares."

"You said you would give us the shares. Those were your words, Jerry."

"Do you expect me to give you something for nothing? You're getting a business worth four or five million rand and you're telling me you want it for nothing?"

"Yes, Jerry. That was the deal."

"Well, the deal's off, Tony."

Tony felt the blood flow into the muscles of his chest. His arms felt twice their normal size. He walked around the desk and grabbed Jerry by the front of his shirt. He lifted him out of the chair.

"You lousy, fucking, two-timing bastard."

Jerry squirmed in his grip, pushed against his chest. Tony raised his left hand, the fingers tightly fisted, and smashed it into Jerry's mouth. He let go Jerry's shirt and the man sprawled to the floor, clutching his bleeding face.

"You can stick your fucking factory up your arse."

Tony turned and walked away.

He drove home and sat in his car for a long time. He wanted his own business. He was going to have his own business. He had no credit record with the banks here in South Africa and he didn't want to use his own money to start his new business. He needed an overdraft, working capital. He needed an investor or someone who would guarantee him at the bank.

Tony jumped out of the car, pushed the door closed. He went inside and dropped his keys on the table in the hall. He opened the study door and sat down at the desk. It was identical to the one he'd had in Zimbabwe and he ran his hand along the burgundy leather inset. The soft texture contrasted with the cool hard feel of the mahogany surround. Tony picked up the phone and dialled Jack's number. He told Jack what had happened with Jerry that morning.

"If you want to stay, Jack, that's up to you, but I'm going to start up again in Turffontein. We've got the warehouse there, we've got the two trucks we stopped from going back to Zim."

"Where will you get the capital, Tony?"

"I'm going to ask Barney Palance to guarantee an overdraft."

"You saved him a lot of money, Tony. I'm sure he'll do it. Give me a couple of weeks, I'll speak to the best of the blokes here and see if they want to join us in Turffontein."

Chapter
Twenty-six

In 1983 the killings began in Zimbabwe. A force recruited from ex-ZANLA guerrillas and trained by North Korean instructors began to hunt down 'dissidents'. They were called the Fifth Brigade and so began a reign of terror.

The Fifth Brigade searched Joshua Nkomo's house in March. Three members of the household died that evening. His property was smashed and vehicles damaged. Nkomo was away with relatives at the time and it was determined that he should go into exile, as his life was in danger. He crossed the border into Botswana and then flew to London.

In Johannesburg, Tony took a phone call from his former receptionist, Pixie. She wondered if he would speak to Herbert Ushuwekunze.

"He's high up in government, Tony; maybe he can sort out this warrant for your arrest. We really miss you at the factory."

"Get him to phone me, Pixie."

The first call from Herbert Ushuwekunze came two days later.

"I'd like to meet with you, Mr Meyer. There are things I need to discuss with you and maybe I can help with your problem."

"That would be fine. Come down to Johannesburg and we can talk."

"I can't come to South Africa. You must come here."

"No, I'm not prepared to return to Zimbabwe. There's a warrant of arrest out for me."

"We can meet at Beit Bridge, Mr Meyer. Customs House."

"As long as it's in South Africa."

"You'll have to come to Zimbabwe Customs House."

"I'm not prepared to cross the border."

"Well, why don't we meet on the bridge itself?"

Tony pushed against the high back of his chair and felt it recline. He lay back and looked at the light fitting in the ceiling. The two spots faced away from each other, one lighting the display of ancient armoury on the wall beside his desk, the other picking out the detail in the large oil painting on the opposite wall. The pastoral scene was painted in the style of the English masters and was a soothing study of the Georgian era.

"Herbert, I'm not going to stand in the middle of the bridge and talk to you. You could have blokes there with rifles who'll take me out. If you really want to meet me then I'll fly to Swaziland. It's neutral territory."

"I'll get back to you, Mr Meyer."

Tony leaned over to replace the telephone on the desk. He picked up his diary and a pen and circled the date. Then he put his hands behind his head and leaned back in the chair. He closed his eyes and hoped the telephone would stay quiet for the next ten minutes.

Herbert Ushuwekunze called a week later to say that Comrade Mugabe wouldn't allow him to travel to Swaziland.

"Well, Herbert, the only other place I can suggest is the international transit lounge at Jan Smuts Airport."

"I'll see what I can do."

Tony had a final phone call from Herbert Ushuwekunze. It seemed that Robert Mugabe would not allow him that option, either. Tony made it clear that he would not return to Zimbabwe under any circumstances.

Q: Do you think it was a set-up? Was he following Mugabe's orders?

A: I don't know, but I wasn't going to risk it. I understand why Pixie got involved with Ushuwekunze—he gave her a good home and security. I'm sure if it was a set-up she knew nothing about it.

Q: Why did they want you back so badly? Didn't they seize all your assets? What use were you to them?"

A: With all the trouble at the time, I think they may have been looking to grab hold of me to give evidence against Joshua Nkomo. At first, when the treason charges were trumped up, I thought it was to do with getting money out of the country—they wanted to stop me and know whom I was assisting. But then the trouble with Nkomo started. So who knows?

Q: I'm not that familiar with Zimababwe's history. Nkomo was part of the government of national unity but then his party was accused of plotting a coup?

A: Nkomo was an N'debele, the minority tribe in Zimbabwe. During the years of Ian Smith's Rhodesian Front he formed the political party—ZAPU. Mugabe, who is Shona, split from the party and formed ZANU. Joshua operated ZAPU out of Zambia, after he was freed from detention in 1974. Both Mugabe's ZANU and Joshua's ZAPU fought the Rhodesian government but they were never allies.

When the Lancaster House accord was signed and elections were held, Nkomo's party lost to Mugabe. But there were strong rumours at the time that the elections were rigged. Mugabe had threatened the British that if he did not win the elections, he would carry on the war until he won completely.

Q: But when you were helping Joshua to sell his country's 'gifts' he was in government?

A: Yes, he was the Minsiter of Home Affairs but then in 1982, ZAPU was accused on plotting a coup, Nkomo was fired and his passport taken away. He had formed an army in the Gwaai valley, about two hundred kilometres south of Victoria Falls. He had a highly organized military operation in place, with plenty of ammunition. His plan was to move into Salisbury and oust Mugabe. Around that time I was helping him furnish his farm in the Matopos region. I asked him what was stopping him from overthrowing Mugabe. He said he was afraid of the Air Force. The Zimbabwean Air Force was still intact from its days as the Rhodesian Air Force and stationed at Thornhill air base in Gweru. He was dead scared of them. I offered to find some good pilots in South Africa who would join the Zimababwean Air Force. We could pay them good money not to take off and fight. But by then the whole thing was over.

Q: You mean the attempted coup was thwarted?

Q: Joshua did not have enough money to feed his soldiers. One of the soldiers came and asked him for money. Being told there was no money and seeing the luxury Nkomo was living in, I imagine the guy was pretty pissed off. He ratted to the Mugabe government. Then the civil war broke out. Government forces killed thousands of people living in Matabeleland.

Q: But he joined the government again, in the late eighties?

A: Well, they wanted an end to the fighting, so they made Joshua a vice-president, which was lucky for me.

Q: Were you able to return to Zimbabwe then?

A: No, but he was able to do me a great favour. In the early nineties, Renée's son was doing some wheeling and dealing. He was caught at Beit Bridge with gold bars under the seat of his car. He was arrested at Customs, tied up and transported two hundred kilometres to Bulawayo with nothing but shorts and a T-shirt. His wife called Renée and she went ballistic—she was in a terrible state. I phoned Nkomo. He asked Renée to meet him in Harare at the Parliament buildings. Soon after that her son was released. He did that for me; he was a friend.

Chapter
Twenty-seven

Meyerton Industries continued to operate under limited production until the money in the company bank accounts ran out. It then quietly closed down, relieving the three hundred and eighty-strong workforce of their means of survival.

In June, Tony approached Palace Shipping and Forwarding with a business plan. The shippers agreed to guarantee a one-million-rand overdraft for Tony's new business, MeySA Limited. The factory opened in a warehouse in Turffontein and began producing the most popular items from Tony's Zimbabwean range of furniture. Tony called Jimmy in Zimbabwe.

"Jimmy, I've started up down here, I need a good accountant. Would you consider making the move?"

"Thanks for the offer Tony, but no thanks. I'll give you a number though. Call Reg Furstenburg. What he doesn't know about bookkeeping isn't worth knowing."

Reg Furstenburg arrived at Tony's office a few days later. He arranged his small neat frame on the visitor's chair, crossed his legs, and tugged his shirt cuffs out from the sleeves of his close-fitting grey suit.

"So, Reg, I hear from Jimmy that you're a very clever man."

"He said the same about you."

"Then we should understand each other without too much effort."

Reg smoothed his pencil moustache, rested his finger in the small cleft of his chin. Tony leaned forward over the desk, looked into the dark eyes of the other man.

"I never sign contracts, Reg. I don't like paperwork."

"Leave too much of that lying about and it gets you into trouble, Tony."

"I work on the fourteen-year principle. Seven lean years, seven good years."

"It's the only way to go."

"The lean years always seem to be very, very lean. The good years only just get the company on its feet."

"I know exactly what you mean, Tony."

"Interested in spending fourteen years with MeySA, Reg?"

"I think I just found my new home."

The business grew and within a year Tony added a mezzanine level to the warehouse in order to double the floor area. He encouraged direct sales through a series of newspaper adverts and displayed the range of products in home-like settings in the small showroom at the factory. The public was pleased to be able to buy from the factory on a cash basis. Cash sales were never deposited at the bank but were distributed among the directors and staff at the end of every month.

Reg Furstenburg gave the taxman exactly what he expected to see in the first years of a new company—huge losses and a growing overdraft. Ronnie produced a monthly income statement for the shippers. Palance Shipping and Forwarding could see that the company was growing at a great pace. The cash sales were declared on the statement and Barney Palance knew that the money was paid to the directors and staff. He didn't care how MeySA Limited presented their books as long as he knew he would never be liable for the overdraft. The income statement that he saw every month showed a very healthy company.

As the workload increased Jack's health began to decline. The years of worry in Zimbabwe had left him with an ulcerated stomach; copious amounts of alcohol had damaged his liver and his smoker's lungs functioned poorly on their diminished capacity. His health problems had exacerbated his nervousness and he slid into a chronic depression. He was admitted to Tara Hospital, a mental facility in Johannesburg.

A couple of months later *The Citizen* newspaper ran a brief report of the death of Jack Moseley, while in the care of Tara Hospital. It was their third suicide that year.

Chapter
Twenty-eight

By June of 1996, Tony's business was in trouble, in spite of some heavy investment from an old friend, Harry Feinstein. The company's bankers called, wanting a little chat. They were getting nervous—MeySA Limited owed them too much money and there was no way of paying it back immediately, despite the five million rand monthly turnover.

The business itself was not in any trouble; in fact it was growing faster than the cash-flow forecasts. But faster growth meant more staff and more money needed to be ploughed back into the business. There simply was not enough excess cash to pay the five hundred thousand rand monthly interest bill. The real problem was that that bill was increasing. Interest rates were climbing and banks were running scared about their mounting bad debts.

The smart-arse banker in his charcoal suit and red tie gave Tony an edgy smile.

"Mr Meyer, we want to know how you suggest meeting your obligations to us … or we are going to have to foreclose."

Tony felt the rage pumping through his body. "What the hell do you want from me? This?" He screamed as he pulled off his shirt.

The shocked faces of the well-groomed gentlemen before him only angered him more.

"Maybe you just want everything," he yelled as he pulled down his pants. "Is this enough yet? It's all I have," he shouted as he kicked off his shoes.

The smart-arse managed to regain his composure before Tony got to his underpants. "Mr Meyer, please calm down. Let's talk about this. What is your solution?"

"Give me a moratorium on the interest payments for a year or two. The payments are preventing me from expanding the business. It's the best chance you have of getting your money back."

The bankers seemed undecided but the thought of seeing Tony butt-naked seemed to sway them.

"Okay, here's the deal. We'll send one of our own guys to look at your accounts and business model. We'll decide if it is worth keeping your business afloat."

Tony's gut feel was that the bank was not going to go for it and he didn't trust the accountant. He gave his son a call. "Craig, you're in the business. I want you to put a tap on this jerk's phone."

Every evening Tony went through the recorded conversations. So he knew when the liquidation order was coming.

They had to act quickly. Tony and some of the other directors had already started to move equipment out of the factory to start another business. A lifelong friend had offered him two million to start over. It was the only way Tony could keep his head above water.

One chilly Friday morning in August, while the frost was still covering the grass, making his drive to work look like a winter wonderland, he got the call that would push him over the edge and turn him into a murderer.

"Tony? It's Will here. I have some not-such-good news. I have heard that your new partner, Harry Feinstein, is doing a dirty on you. He's has gone and set up with some other guys and is starting to manufacture some of your furniture."

Although Harry flatly denied it at first, Tony soon found out that he had indeed set up a new business, taking with him the most popular lines that MeySA were selling.

Tony had never been so angry. "That fucking little shit. He has gone behind my back; he has ruined me—I'm going to have to sort him out."

Tony's hand shook so much he struggled to dial Mike's number. Mike was the kind of guy you called when you needed some dirty work done. He worked for an elite force within the South African Police and had no compunction in using his position to screw people over.

"Mike, I need you to help me remove someone from the face of the earth. I'll make it worth your while."

Tony and Mike set out the plan. It was brilliant—no one would ever find the body. The night before Harry was to meet his maker, Mike called.

"I can't do this—prison for a cop is no joke."

"You know, you are all brawn and bravado but you have the heart of a fucking chicken, Mike. Just one word of warning, if you try to blackmail me I'll have you sorted too."

Tony slammed down the phone. He was a big guy and he worked out—little Harry Feinstein would be no problem. He would go ahead with it regardless.

Tony knew Harry went for a jog every morning. He left really early, around six o' clock when there was little traffic on the road. His tight hold on the purse strings had pushed his wife to pack her bags several years ago. He lived alone, so no one would miss him … for a while.

Tony waited at the top of a sleep slope. He knew Harry's route and he knew Harry was practically spitting out his lungs by the time he reached the top. Just like an old 'skop-skiet-en-donder' movie, he clubbed Harry across his temple with a baseball bat and dragged him to a nearby clump of trees, where a truck was parked, packed with the necessary equipment. He bound Harry from head to toe with duck tape. Wrapped up like a mummy—within one hour Harry would stop breathing.

Tony waited until late evening before he dared make the drive to the Vaal Dam. Making sure to avoid speed-trap cameras clicking away at his number plate, he drove carefully below the speed limit and arrived at the dam wall in just under an hour.

He climbed into the back of the truck and felt to check that the cement he had poured over Harry had hardened sufficiently. Then he wrapped a large truck-tyre rubber tube around the body and finally rolled it up in a large fishing net. He jumped out of the back of the truck and looked around. It was quiet. A weeknight—not many visitors to the dam. He backed the truck up as close as he could get to the wall. He walked around to the back where he had positioned the body close to the tailgate. With a deep breath, summoning every ounce of his strength, he pulled the body out through the doors and, with a grunt, heaved the corpse over wall.

The body was never found. Between the fishing net, tubing and cement the fish never got to it.

Tony starts fiddling with the letter opener lying on his desk. He turns it over and over between his fingers.

Q: You look uncomfortable. Do you regret it?

A: He was a little shit, got what he deserved.

Q: Earlier you said talking about it was tricky.

A: Yes, well, I am admitting to murder. It's in the book.

Q: Did it really happen?

Tony turns his head to look out the window. He starts tapping the letter opener against his desk to a rhythmic beat that is playing out in his head.

Chapter
Twenty-nine

In December 1997, MeySA Limited was put into liquidation. The financers were out of pocket for a cool twenty-one million rand and they were looking to get back whatever they could.

Tony had to start selling his assets but his properties, thank God, were safe in Renée's name. Over the years, when Tony was bringing money out of Zimbabwe as part of his currency-exchange scheme, he had used the cash to buy property in South Africa. In those days agents and sellers didn't ask too many questions and you could pay with cash. Knowing the Zimbabwean government would be keeping a close eye on him, Tony put Renée's name on the title deeds.

Now that the liquidators were breathing hard down his neck he thanked his lucky stars for this extra protection. It was all he had left from the millions he had accrued over the years. The properties belonged to Renée and they could not touch them ... he hoped.

But he was still nervous. It was this insecurity that led him to make his most stupid and, by far, most expensive mistake. He was sitting at his desk in his cluster home in Johannesburg's northern suburbs, going through bank statements and cash flows that he had to hand over to the liquidators, when his phone rang.

"Honey. it's me."

"Hi doll, how's the weather in Knysna?"

"Great. I miss you. When can you come down?"

"Not for a while. I'm up to my ears trying to sort out this whole bloody mess."

"Well, actually that's why I'm calling. I met with my lawyer today. You've met him—Frank Kruger."

"Tall guy with a beard?"

"Yes, that's him. Well, he has an idea to ensure that the properties stay out of reach of the liquidators, but I'm not sure you're going to like it."

"Look, I'm not in much of a position to argue. What does he suggest?"

"He said it would be best if we got divorced … just for appearances. Then you would have no claim on the properties and nor would the liquidators."

Tony started to fiddle with his letter opener; it had become a nervous habit over the last couple of hellish months.

"Renée, it seems wrong. We married for better or for worse."

"Yes, but we will know it's just for show; it will change nothing. I will stay down here at our holiday home until it all blows over and then we can re-marry."

Tony sighed. "Okay, doll. Should I fly down to sign the papers?"

"That will be great. They are ready and waiting." Renée's voice took on a husky edge, "We can say farewell in style."

The next day Tony caught a flight to George, before driving the fifty kilometres to his beautiful holiday home on the Knysna coastline. As the Knysna heads came into view his heart sank with the thought that he would not be able to return here for sometime. He was going to miss Renée terribly. She was his rock, the only person he trusted. She had been so brave and courageous and helped him out of more tight spots than he could actually remember.

As he pulled up at their home, actually her home now, Renée was waiting on the steps outside the front door.

To his surprise she quickly jumped in the car. "Frank is waiting for us. We may as well get it over and done with."

"I thought we could have a few moments together. I'm still struggling with the idea."

"I know, but Frank could only see us now. We'll have lunch together afterwards."

Sitting in front of the massive mahogany desk, with a wildlife painting by Gordon Vorster hanging on the wall behind the lawyer, Tony signed the papers.

"How long do you think we will have to keep up this pretence, Frank?"

"One year, tops."

It was going to be a long, lonely year.

He made love to Renée for the last time in their, no, make that her bedroom, with the view over the ocean. Renée seemed distracted, which was understandable but when he saw a school of dolphins skimming the crests of the waves he took it as a good sign. He kissed her forehead. "It will be okay, doll."

But it wasn't. From that moment on it was never ever going to be okay again. Within a few months Tony realized that Renée was not going to re-marry him. Maybe at the time, when the lawyer concocted this crazy idea, she really did believe it was temporary. But as the months passed she got used to living without Tony. Actually, she started to enjoy her independence. She could spend her money as she wished— a monthly income of over seventy-six thousand rand from her eight properties meant a very healthy bank balance and a lavish lifestyle.

Tony was totally ruined but he did not dare go to lawyers; after all, the properties had been bought with ill-gotten gains. Anything that he owned had been taken by the bank.

He had to sell all his eleven cars.

He still has models of them in his study. Beautiful imported cars like the American Excalibur. The models are first class—the doors open, steering wheels turn and you can even open the bonnets to look at the miniature engines.

But the models are all that is left now … and a painting of Renée and him. But even that is about to be auctioned.

Q: Why?

A: My new wife refuses to have it in the house. I don't blame her. The painting is very erotic … Renée and I … naked in our boudoir.

Q: Are you angry with Renée, bitter?

A: Tony shrugs his shoulders. I feel hurt, but that's life.

Q: You mentioned though, that you thought she'd been having affairs during your marriage?

A: One I know of—with Al Capone's nephew—of all people—when we used to visit New York. She couldn't resist power and money. But I got over it … after all, I was hardly an angel either.

Q: What's happened to her now?

A: I still see her from time to time. I was at her brother's funeral this afternoon. She's not a well woman—something to do with her stomach—it's bubbling, eating her up from the inside.